D1053652

The Lightning Field

THE
LIGHTNING
FIELD

Travels In and Around New Mexico

Robert Eaton

Johnson Books
Boulder

For Marty

9 8 7 6 5 4 3 2 1

"Adobe Plains" appeared in slightly different form in the *High Plains Literary Review*, Spring 1994.

Cover design by Margaret Donharl
Cover photograph of the moonrise over Hernandez, New Mexico, and the Sangre de Cristo Range by Stephen Trimble.

Library of Congress Cataloging-in-Publication Data

Eaton, Robert, 1954–
    The lightning field : travels in and around New Mexico / Robert Eaton.
        p.   cm.
    Includes bibliographical references (p.   ).
    ISBN 1-55566-153-X (hardcover : alk. paper). -- ISBN 1-55566-159-9 (paperback : alk. paper)
    1. New Mexico--Description and travel.   2. Navajo Indians.
I. Title.
F801.2.E28   1995
917.8904'53--dc20   95-19366
                                           CIP

Printed in the United States by
Johnson Printing
1880 South 57th Court
Boulder, Colorado 80301

Printed on recycled paper with soy ink.

CONTENTS

PART I

PART II

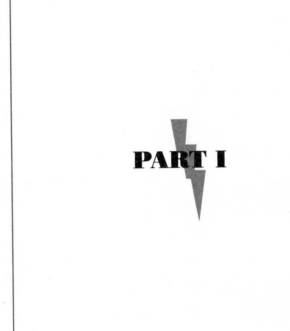

PART I

The Lightning Field

The Dia Art Foundation is a nonprofit corporation chartered in New York State in 1974 and dedicated to "the planning, realization and presentation of important works of contemporary art." It seeks "projects of a scale and originality not supported by existing institutions in the society." The foundation maintains several offices and galleries in Manhattan, as well as an office in Quemado, New Mexico, population 250.

The terms of the contract are many and precise. We are to meet at the foundation's Quemado office at 1:00 PM on the day of our reservation. We will be transported to the site in the foundation's truck and must remain there for twenty-four hours. Cameras are not permitted. Although six people may visit the site simultaneously, each may be previously acquainted with no more than two of the others. Food and sleeping accommodations will be provided. Neither the foundation nor its employees are responsible for any injury that may occur during our stay. Our checks should be made payable to the Dia Art Foundation.

August 19 is a bright, breezy day in western New Mexico. We approach Quemado from the south, dropping out of Apache National Forest onto an arid plain. In Spanish *quemado* means "burned," and this land does indeed look seared. The grasses are withered, and the gnarled juniper trees look as if they're still grimacing from the fire. The town itself is a sleepy ranching community, with its business district—a post office, a couple of gas stations, and a general mercantile—strung along the highway. The Dia Art Foundation has moved into an unmarked, rundown building in the middle of town. We park out front and walk through the door into a different world.

The interior is in a state of anarchic renovation. The hardwood floors are being refinished, the walls are being repainted, and the main floor space has recently been subdivided into galleries, in the largest of which sits an amoeboid modernist sculpture. Other people—a foundation employee and our fellow guests—are there, and the air is thick with talk of "utilization of space" and "plasticity of form." We are the last to arrive, and the foundation employee, a personable, talkative woman named Audrey Ward, soon directs us into the front office for final instructions.

By the time we step outdoors again, the foundation's truck, a four-wheel-drive GMC king cab with tandem rear wheels, is waiting for us, and so is Buck, our driver, a laconic, tobacco-chewing man in cowboy hat and manure-stained boots not in the least prone to talk of "plasticity of form." As we load our bags into the truck, I ask Buck if he's from Quemado.

"Nope," he says in a ranch drawl. "Pietown." He pauses a minute, then adds, "But I live here now."

With that we are ready to go. The day is lovely, so Becky and I and another couple—they graduate students in whatnot at the University of New Mexico, we erstwhile, reformed students—decide to ride in back, open to glorious sun and sky.

Buck blasts north out of town on the highway to Zuni. We attempt conversation for a few minutes before giving up, the wind roaring in our ears. About fifteen miles later we turn east on what the maps call New Mexico 36, a rutted, washboarded dirt road. Heedless of the terrain, Buck maintains his speed. We begin to shift uncomfortably, our coccyges taking quite a beating on the metal bed of the truck. Fortunately, we soon take a cutoff to the north, the road worsens, and even Buck must slow down. Every couple of hundred yards the road now dissolves into a watery mud hole, a product of the afternoon thundershowers common at this time of year. At each fetid water hole a group of cows impassively observes our progress.

Since turning off the paved highway, we have been making our way slowly toward the middle of a vast, uninhabited plain ringed by low, serrate mountains. Except for a few scrubby junipers, the plain is devoid of trees. It is a startlingly exposed landscape. I'm beginning to wonder if we're on the right road when we encounter a locked gate with a "No Trespassing" sign posted con-spicuously on it. Buck gets out and opens it and we con-tinue slowly, driving around the mud holes when we can, otherwise churning through them.

It appears gradually, first a few of the poles pok-ing over a rise, then a few more, finally the entire array. The poles are so slender that when they're not glinting in the sun or silhouetted against the sky, they blend into the background, invisible. Their appearance and disap-pearance is strangely unsettling.

I've been curious about our accommodations, and now ahead of us, on the north edge of the site, I see a small cabin, its rustic quality enhanced by its proximity to the steely array. Buck pulls up to a door facing away from the site and we stand and stretch and climb out, glad the ride is over. We've traveled about thirty-five miles in an hour.

The cabin is an old homesteader's place that has been renovated and enlarged. The original structure was sturdy and well built, but I also admire the quality of the recent work, the tightly caulked log walls and snugly jointed window frames. I ask Buck if he did the work, and he nods and says, "Yep." Inside, through the kitchen, a common area with rough-hewn furniture con-nects to a bathroom, two bedrooms, and a porch with weathered wooden rocking chairs overlooking the array. On the east side of the cabin a third bedroom enjoys a private entrance. The kitchen is well stocked with dishes and silverware, pots and pans, and food of a nutritious, supermarket variety: fresh fruits, eggs, whole wheat bread, peanut butter. The cabin has electricity and running water, unexpected amenities here in the middle of nowhere. Buck explains that the local cooperative supplies the electricity through a line buried for the last mile to the cabin and that a water well and submersible pump are concealed behind a low rise to the northwest. We unload the bags, Buck tells us he'll be back in a couple of hours, and he's gone, leaving us alone to contemplate the *objet* before us.

The Lightning Field, according to a pamphlet supplied by the Dia Art Foundation, is a "permanent earth sculpture" created by Walter De Maria, an avant-garde New York sculptor known for his "minimalist land art." The pamphlet provides the following deadpan description of the project: "A permanent earth sculpture. One mile by one kilometer, 400 stainless steel poles, with solid stainless steel pointed tips, arranged in a rectangular grid array (sixteen poles wide by twenty-five poles long) spaced 220 feet (67.07 meters) apart. Pole tips form an even plane. Average pole height is twenty feet seven inches (6.27 meters)." This array of projectiles was completed in 1977. If one were of a Freudian turn of mind, one would want to know more about Mr. De Maria.

The Lightning Field is a clever name, calling to mind electrical fields in physics and conjuring images of lightning arcing between poles as charges build up on them, but it is something of a misnomer. The poles can act as lightning rods, but they do not cause lightning or act as capacitors. This part of New Mexico, known as the North Plains, is naturally one of the most lightning-active spots in North America, which may help explain the name Quemado and the absence of trees here at 7,200 feet. No, the poles do not cause lightning. What they do is reflect light, whether its source is lightning, the sun, or the moon. Against a background of black, roiling storm clouds rived by bolts of lightning, the silvery poles are especially dramatic, but they also reflect sunlight at various times on clear days, notably sunrise and sunset, and moonlight on clear nights.

With Buck gone, Becky and I explore the cabin in earnest. We are impressed with the bathroom, equipped with a flush toilet and full-sized bathtub. Behind a wall panel in the common area we discover a narrow staircase to a cramped attic loft, evidently Walter De Maria's private domain; on the bed lie some notes concerning construction of the array. Back downstairs we peruse the guest register (dominated by New Mexicans and New Yorkers) and copies of recent articles about the project from *Artforum* and *Art Journal* (the former a technical fact sheet and statement of aesthetic principles authored by De Maria himself; the latter a rather highbrow affair which discusses, among other things, "Hussey's seven attributes of the sublime"). We then stake a claim on a bedroom and, finally, wander outside into the array itself.

I should confess right here that I have no interest in cognitive theories of art or explanations of what an artist is trying to do. When I read or hear about "conceptual frameworks" and "modes of intentionality," my eyes glaze over and my mind begins to search frantically for a way out. Abstract nouns give me the willies. I like art, am drawn to it for personal, idiosyncratic reasons—one of which is simply that some art gives me great pleasure—but as far as explaining a work of art, my feeling is that, as the saying goes, the proof is in the pudding. A work of art should not have to be explained to be enjoyed or appreciated. It should attack us viscerally, excite our senses, set our minds on fire. Or maybe just help us through the day.

The Lightning Field is an impressive sculpture, an eerie place. Its appeal is, at least initially, the appeal of science fiction; namely, the fascination of the unknown. For a little while we are kids again, thrilling to our imaginations. We are space travelers plunked down in the middle of a mysterious metal array obviously designed by some superior intelligence. What is it and who made it? Is its creator here somewhere, observing us? Is he toying with us? Are we soon going to hear all around us a laugh like the ominous laugh of the abominable Dr. Phibes? Ah-ha-ha-ha . . .

We walk up to one of the poles. Its surface is a satiny, convex mirror, smooth and cool to the touch. With one hand I can almost encircle it. I'd hate to have to shimmy up one of these things. I grab hold of it with both hands and try to shake it. There is enough flexibility in the steel or enough give in the ground that I can cause it to vibrate slightly. According to De Maria's fact sheet, each pole is anchored in three feet of concrete, and the top of each concrete foundation is buried a foot underground. I think about digging 400 four-foot-deep holes and setting each pole in the ground in its proper position. How did De Maria ensure that the tips of the poles form a plane? Surveyors on ladders? Twenty-five feet of stainless steel pole with solid tip must weigh quite a bit. And cost quite a lot. What was the budget for this project anyway? (The fact sheet scrupulously omits that information.) And what do the ranchers in the area, the neighbors, think about this extravagant example of 3-D techno-art and the small groups of strange people who come to visit it?

Glancing at the ground, I spot a small potsherd, which I pick up and study. It is of a variety called Tularosa black-on-white, probably made a thousand years ago by Pueblo Indians who inhabited the Rio Grande valley east of here. Surely none of those Indians lived on the North Plains. I try to imagine why they would have been traveling through here—going where and for what?—and why they would have been carrying a pot. Carrying their water across this arid expanse? Someone dropped this pot, broke it. In surprise? For a minute my sense of time is confused, and I imagine the Indians staring in awe at the array, then perhaps averting their eyes and whispering protective incantations. Not a bad idea. This place does inspire a certain fearful reverence. Then again, perhaps this pot wasn't a water vessel at all; perhaps the Indians came deliberately to the high plain surrounded by distant mountains, carrying in the pot an offering of blue-corn meal for the kachinas, the rain-power beings, who reside here, entreating them to come to the valley below with clouds and moisture, thunder and lightning.

As we wander through the array, we notice a lot of varmint holes, most of them dug by rabbits probably, although prairie dogs and badgers are also possibilities. Peering into one that looks to have been abandoned long ago, we see a black widow spider with two cottony eggs suspended in a cloud of web. Even had I never seen a black widow before, I would somehow sense that this spider is dangerous. She is an eight-legged Darth Vader. A primordial fear shudders through my body. But I am fascinated as well. Wondering what her reaction will be, I gently prod her with the end of a long stem of grass, and she retreats out of sight down the hole, only to reappear a minute later to cuddle her eggs and nimbly carry them back down with her. It seems that everywhere we look today we see something marvelous.

We finally decide to return to the cabin, where our compatriots have roosted. Much to my dismay, the graduate students are sitting in the rockers on the porch discussing De Maria's concept of "the piece." There is talk of how the array "inhabits its space" and how it "interacts with its environment." We perch on the steps, and Becky, bless her heart, produces a flask from which I quickly take a couple of intemperate slugs. Their effect is immediate. The conversation behind us suddenly seems . . . well, not fatuous, but silly, hilarious even. I begin to punctuate it randomly with giggles and have soon degenerated into paroxysms of laughter. It's catching, and Becky begins to lose control too. We are embarrassed but unable to stop. Fortunately, the couple behind us chooses not to associate our deviant behavior with their conversation. They merely regard us with wan, tolerant smiles. I finally excuse myself, go for a walk, and return a few minutes later in a more composed state.

For the rest of the afternoon we sit quietly on the porch, watching the clouds build over the mountains to the south, watching the array for signs of change. One of the other men, of an even baser sort than I, has decided that he would like to touch all four hundred of the poles, so he is jogging slowly back and forth in front of us, weaving his way silently to the far edge. His movement is slow and deliberate and so constant as to be almost mesmerizing. He seems to be jogging to the rhythm of the day. A metronomical calm descends on us as we sit on the porch, waiting for afternoon to attenuate into evening. A light breeze noiselessly stirs the grass. There is no sound, save for the occasional twitter of a small bird navigating through the spindly steel forest, and those occasional twitters only call attention to the absence of sound. In the middle of the North Plains we come to know the silence of space.

A tensile regiment . . . Four hundred very large knitting needles stuck in the ground . . . A giant bed of nails for a gargantuan swami. This place is eerie, surreal. (Those craggy ridges behind the array must be the Sawtooth Mountains, about twenty miles south. On the other side of them is an expanse of arid grassland known as the Plains of San Agustín, with another futuristic project in the middle of it. That one, known as the Very Large Array, consists of twenty-seven large-dish radio antennas positioned along a Y-shaped system of railroad tracks, each arm of the Y extending thirteen miles. It probes the universe on behalf of the federal government.) I imagine the array just before sunset or just after sunrise, when each of the silvery poles casts a supernaturally long black shadow, and I can't help thinking of the Italian surrealist Giorgio de Chirico and his chiaroscuro paintings of statue-like figures in stark, empty piazzas. This place shares with those paintings a certain mood: otherworldly, premonitory, mute. The difference is that the paintings are fixed, static, incapable of change, whereas the array is in flux, always reflecting or translating what is going on around it. An hour before sunset or an hour after sunrise it looks different. Even on a clear afternoon it changes subtly from minute to minute. I am intrigued by this discovery. (I wonder if this is what that couple meant with their talk of "interacting with the environment"? Perhaps I should ask them? No.) I look at the cloudless sky overhead. We won't get any lightning today, but we can still look forward to the drama of sunset.

Our afternoon reverie is interrupted only by the return of Buck with our dinner, a lasagna casserole his wife has baked. After he delivers it to the kitchen, I walk with him outside and, as he is climbing in the truck, ask him what he thinks of the array. He shifts the position of the quid in his cheek with his tongue and looks at the ground pensively, mulling his answer. Mustn't antagonize the customers.

"I guess it's okay," he says finally.

Back in the cabin Becky and I greedily eat our portion of the casserole, which is delicious, and return to the porch to resume our watch.

13

Sunset is disappointing. Late in the afternoon a wave of slate-colored clouds washes in over the western horizon, and the sun sinks into it without so much as a fizzle. But a peculiar thing happens anyway: the poles dissolve magically in the gray light of dusk. One minute they are there, silhouetted against a pale salmon sky, and the next minute they are gone and we are looking at an empty plain. Again the effect is strangely unsettling. I am tempted to walk out into that murky space to make sure they're still there. This would not be a good place for a paranoid to spend a vacation.

A magnificent New Mexican night, suffused with starlight, envelops us. Unfortunately, the moon will not rise until long after midnight and we are tired cowboys, so we retire early, falling into a deep, comfortable sleep untroubled by dreams of impalement. The night passes quickly, and when we awake, the sun has already cleared the horizon. The morning is bright and dewy, surprisingly springlike at this elevation. Little kids should be skipping to school today. The array is still there, or it's back, and it seems oddly familiar. We aren't overwhelmed by its novelty and strangeness as we were yesterday. In fact, this morning there is a comforting sameness about it. (Perhaps, I'm thinking, the array is more than a phantasm. Perhaps it obeys natural laws after all.) Despite its familiarity, though, its beauty remains undiminished. In the early sun the sides of the poles gleam like icicles on Christmas morning.

Before we came, I was suspicious of the condition that we must spend twenty-four hours at the site. I didn't understand the reasons for it then, as I think I do now, and I didn't like the idea that we would be stranded at this place overnight, unable to leave even if we wanted to. But my doubts have been assuaged. In fact, this morning I'm thinking that I wouldn't mind staying here for a week or two or three. The cabin is secure and comfortable. It has electricity and running water. It is miles from the nearest telephone. (Hallelujah!) It is in the middle of a glorious expanse of space and air and light. And it has this astonishing, constantly changing, always beautiful thing in its backyard. All we lack are books, music (Miles Davis's *In a Silent Way* for starters), and a supply of good liquor. Why not? And every night Buck could bring us a tasty dinner that the missis has cooked. Yes, life could be good . . .

Becky and I fix a leisurely breakfast, then take a long last walk to the north, away from the array. We are looking for an elevated point from which to view the site, but the topography is too subtle. Our outing is, however, far from disappointing. Walking back to the cabin along a puddle-stained road, we notice swarms of tadpoles in the water, a few already with tiny rear legs. If the puddles last another few weeks, these tadpoles will mature into spadefoot toads. The toads will immediately burrow into the mud and remain there in a state of suspended animation as the ground around them dries and hardens, until next summer's thundershowers call them out to mate and reproduce and fill next year's puddles with tadpoles. If the rains don't come then, the toads will sleep through to the next summer, or the next, all the while, I imagine, subconsciously waiting for that rhythmic tap-tapping on the ground above their heads. If the rains don't come for three or four years, the toads will go through their final metamorphosis without ever waking.

Because of their association with the vital summer rains, the tadpoles have acquired an almost sacred status among the Pueblo Indians, who often decorate their pottery with stylized images of them. Their depiction on the pottery is a way of venerating the animals, now a symbol of water and fertility, and at the same time calling them forth, invoking them and what they represent. Dat ol' mimetic magic. For a minute, surprisingly, I find myself thinking about the array. Does De Maria hope that it will achieve some similar kind of preferred status in the minds of those of us who see it? Will lodge in our psyches, like a basketball that gets stuck between the backboard and rim? Become our tadpoles, so to speak?

By the time we return to the cabin, the morning is spent. We are packing when Buck arrives, half an hour early. He will drive back out to the site with his wife later this afternoon to clean the cabin and prep it for the next group, who will arrive in Quemado tomorrow at 1:00 PM. Our tailbones are sore, but we can't resist the sun, so we climb in back again. The cabin recedes slowly, until it is finally just a matchbox on a sea of plain. As we stare in its direction, the array blends quietly into the background for the last time.

Buck doesn't spare the horses on the drive back, and we are in Quemado in two beats of a hummingbird's wings, as they say in these parts. Audrey flutters out to greet us.

"Isn't the piece fantastic?" she asks.

We agree that it is. We thank Buck for his patience with our questions, and he actually looks a little embarrassed, as if he's going to say, "Aw shucks, it was nothin'." But he just nods. We get into the car and drive slowly east, bound for the Datil Diner. It's supposed to serve the best green-chile chicken enchiladas in this part of the state.

Chaco Canyon

I leave Albuquerque in the late heat of a June afternoon, driving north toward Santa Fe below the rugged escarpment of the Sandia Mountains. At Bernalillo I turn northwest on New Mexico 44—heavy with truck traffic, one of New Mexico's deadliest highways—cross the Rio Grande, and climb out of the valley through sandy, juniper-speckled hills. Ahead the Jemez Mountains lie like a dark body across the desert sky, in one shoulder the ulcerous gash of a red-rock canyon. The highway descends to the mouth of the canyon, then skirts the mountains to the south and west, climbing through colored clay hills and crumbling sandstone mesas onto the Colorado Plateau, that high, arid tableland incised by great rivers that stretches away into Colorado, Arizona, and Utah.

Beyond the Hispanic village of Cuba, beyond the pine-studded hills of the continental divide, the highway spills onto the Jicarilla Apache reservation, an immense sea of sage that dips and swells and breaks over small sandstone reefs. The air is cool here, prickling my arm on the open window; the late light ale-colored and liquid. At sunset I pass the gas compressor station at Lybrook, its steely pipes illuminated eerily by floodlights and a wavering orange gas flare.

I'm entering Navajo country now, that sprawling province of mesa and sky that is, even today, foreign to most white Americans. At Nageezi Trading Post, almost three hours out of Albuquerque, I slow and turn south on an unmarked dirt road, and a weathered wooden sign announces, "Chaco Canyon 26 Miles / No Food or Gas Available / Travel at Own Risk When Wet." The road is washboarded and rough, but I know it well and can maintain thirty-five miles per hour most of the way, slowing only for the cattle guards and arroyo crossings and clay-rutted curves. Oil and kerosene lamps twinkle in the hogans and cinder-block houses scattered over the dusky landscape, and a horned owl—a harbinger of death according to the Navajos—flies up suddenly from the road in front of me.

By the time I wind down into the canyon and past the ruins, darkness has settled. I pull up to my trailer and step out of the car. For a minute I stand there dazed, my eyes accustomed to the headlights, my ears roaring with the wind. Only slowly does the world reveal itself. The sky is clear—pale blue on the western horizon, indigo overhead. The stars glitter sharply like ice crystals on a bright November morning. By their light I can make out the dark rim of canyon wall, the shadowy form of talus boulder, the silhouette of Fajada Butte. Beyond the butte a plain stretches away to the southwest, and on the horizon in that direction I can see two globes of light, one cast by the tiny Navajo town of Crownpoint thirty miles away, the other by Gallup forty miles beyond that. Even at night one has here an exhilarating sense of emptiness and space. Small lights burn in the other trailers, but the air is still and I can't help but feel that I am alone in the center of a vast world of rock and sky. The car engine crackles softly as it cools, a reassuring sound in the midst of this silence. I relax and breathe more easily, glad to be home. Alone at night, with the contours of the land softened by darkness, I sometimes think that this is the most beautiful place in the world.

I haven't always felt this way. I still remember the first time I drove into the canyon—more than five years ago now—still remember how discouraged I felt at the prospect of what I saw. In the harsh light of afternoon, with the sun sucking the color out of the sandstone cliffs, the landscape looked bleak and forbidding. I thought then that I would stay for only a short time before going elsewhere, but I learned, before that summer was out, that the canyon seems a different place with the sun low in the sky, or on stormy afternoons, or on quiet, starry nights; and I was intrigued by its changes in aspect and mood. I returned the next year, and the next, and I have come to be fascinated, during my time here, by the canyon's personality and history, by its almost tangible presence, and, most of all, by the strange power it exerts over the people who try to live here. Often these days I find myself thinking about the canyon's first inhabitants, a mysterious people we call the Anasazi, who built beautiful sandstone pueblos here a thousand years ago; they established the pattern, started the sequence of events that has led to the present, the past-laden present, with the canyon now a small national park where I work during the summers, leading tours through the ruins of the villages they abandoned long ago.

No one knows where the Anasazi came from. The archeologists who work here tell me that they probably were descended from the aboriginal people of the Four Corners area, people who, around the time of Christ, began to give up their nomadic way of life as they learned the rudiments of agriculture. They may have been desert nomads, but when they started to farm, they naturally settled in well-watered locations like Mesa Verde and Canyon de Chelly. No one knows what they saw in Chaco or why, a thousand years ago, this desolate canyon developed into their greatest cultural center.

Thousands of people lived here then, and a network of well-maintained roads radiated from the canyon to its satellite communities in the surrounding area. Chaco was a tough place to live, but somehow the Anasazi managed. They planted corn, beans, and squash; gathered piñon nuts and squawbush berries; and hunted the wild game in the area—rabbits, mule deer, pronghorn antelope. Some archeologists believe that they developed a regional food redistribution system to safeguard against famine and that the large pueblos in the canyon—the so-called great houses of Chaco—served as giant warehouses to stockpile food grown in the satellite villages. Whatever the mechanics of the system, the Anasazi in and around the canyon evidently worked together, for a time at least, to ensure their survival in this inhospitable place.

Those of us who work in the park today enjoy accommodations less communal and considerably less grand than the prehistoric pueblos. We live in cinder-block houses, trailers, and prefab apartments near the park's visitor center, and when we need food, we drive seventy-five miles into Farmington, the nearest large town, to the Safeway. Because the park's maintenance crew is composed entirely of local Navajos who commute to work every day from their homes in the surrounding area, the community is small—twenty-five in the summer, ten in the winter—and white.

In the course of conversation visitors sometimes tell me that they would love to live in the canyon. I know they imagine our lives here to be a desert idyll, free of the aggravations and stresses that afflict people in more urban settings. And in some respects they are right, for the canyon can be a beautiful, tranquil place. But they don't anticipate the subtle difficulties of our situation, don't consider that life in this isolated place might exacerbate the personal problems that people bring with them wherever they go. And they certainly don't believe me when I tell them how a year or two here can affect people, what strange behavior some time in Chaco Canyon can produce.

In a recent issue of *The Courier*, the official Park Service newsletter, in a short article heralding his retirement, the superintendent of the park averred that life in the canyon is tough on everyone who lives here, but especially on nonworking wives who must find something to do to fill their days. "I've seen 'em almost carried out of here," he concluded jovially.

It is true. And, understandably perhaps, there have been, in recent history, a couple of legendary hypochondriacs among that group of women. About ten years ago one of the rangers received a hardship transfer out of the canyon because his wife was given to moments of hysteria during which she claimed that her eyeballs were drying out. (Randy, our former park archeologist, delighted in that kind of story, and it was he who discovered the official correspondence concerning that particular case, which he considered a paradigm of sorts.) More recently, another ranger's wife became convinced that she was suffering from a variety of serious diseases during her husband's tour of duty in the canyon. After an acquaintance of hers developed multiple sclerosis, she too began to experience the symptoms. Then she contracted bubonic plague (endemic to the area, so not completely out of the question; but, alas, easily diagnosed) and finally suffered a "dehydrated brain," at which time she claimed that she could feel her gray matter rattling against her skull. They too were transferred to a less isolated park.

The wives aren't alone. Life in the canyon eventually wears down even those who spend their days at the office or in the field, more quickly if they're involved in one of the petty feuds (comical if not so bitter) that seem inevitably to develop between coworkers out here. You simply can't avoid someone you don't like. During my first summer in the canyon one of the female rangers refused to speak to her male counterpart (their personal relationship had come to grief), and we were forced to carry messages back and forth between them even if they were sitting in the same room. They also lived next door to each other.

Like the wives, we also suffer occasionally from too much time and not enough to do. One of my room-mates liked to talk about "massaging" projects at work, by which he meant spending eight hours doing something that required only two or three, because he knew that when he finished, he would have nothing else—or worse, only busy work—to do. The tedium can dull one's judgment, and people who stay here year-round for two or three years tend to lose their perspective on what's important and what isn't and to overreact to minor situations.

Several years ago someone played an ill-advised practical joke on an unpopular ranger, rolling a cherry bomb into his trailer in the middle of the night. Instead of dealing with the incident in a reasonable manner, however, the superintendent and the chief ranger launched a full-blown criminal investigation, collecting "evidence" and tape-recording interrogations of "suspects." (Did the Anasazi ever behave so bizarrely? With such paranoid fanaticism? Is that what finally caused them to abandon the place?) They eventually identified the culprit as one of the other rangers—the wrong person, I later learned—and the superintendent called the state's attorney general to try to prosecute him for arson. At that point the regional office in Santa Fe intervened, and the matter was hastily dropped, though not without hard feelings all around.

After observing that kind of behavior, Randy would shake his head slowly and tamp his pipe and pronounce his theory of Chaco Canyon: "It's the water. It must be the water. Franklin," he would say, referring to the Navajo employee who maintains the park's water treatment plant, "must be putting something in the water."

"You have to laugh at what goes on out here," another friend of mine says. "Otherwise you end up in the shit-can."

And we do laugh, or try to, a small group of us, although, I must admit, our laughter is partly sardonic. It is the kind that comes from reading *Catch-22* or listening to Frank Zappa. Listening to Zappa especially, as when he intones flatly:

> Once upon a time,
> It was in Albuquerque, New Mexico. . . .
> There was nothing [ ] to do.
> It was Albuquerque, New Mexico.

We laugh at the Anasazi, about whom we know very little, but who seem to epitomize the mystery and strangeness of the place; and we laugh at the Navajos, who keep to themselves and who watch us silently from a distance; and, most of all, we laugh at ourselves, the Anglos, the *bilig'aanas*, the crazy white people. We laugh and we talk. It helps us keep our sanity.

"This park runs on screwy oral tradition, backstabbing, and manufactured crises."

"You know why the archeologists can't figure out what was going on here a thousand years ago? Because there wasn't anything going on in this stinking canyon. It was just like it is today."

"People have nothing better to do out here than to get weird."

Given our attitude toward life in the canyon, it may seem surprising that all of us came here by choice initially and that I return by choice every summer. I won't presume to speak for the others, but I can say that this place seems to have a strange hold on me, that I feel myself drawn back to it whenever I leave, and that I am fascinated by life in the canyon, albeit in a morbid way. Perhaps I wouldn't feel as I do if I were facing the prospect of an indefinite amount of time here, numberless winters without relief . . .

Yes, winters are especially tough. Chaco may be in New Mexico, but it is also at 6,200 feet elevation and nighttime temperatures below zero are common in January and February. Nevertheless, the intense sun melts the icy roads at midday, turning them to slop (slicker'n snot on a doorknob, as they say out here), keeping visitors away, and causing you to wonder if you'll ever make it to town again. Telephone service, provided by Navajo Communications Company, is erratic at best, as are television and radio reception. When a bad winter storm moves into the canyon and clouds press down on the mesa tops and snow obliterates the view and the phones go dead and the radio is just scratchy static, then you begin to doubt the reality of that other world of cities and men you've left behind and to look around suspiciously at the people here with whom you've cast your lot. A winter in Chaco Canyon can seriously warp your view of the world.

Not surprisingly, rangers stationed here year-round invariably want to leave after a winter or two, even those who are able to laugh. When our resource management specialist recently got another job in Denver, he received the following celebratory letter from Randy, who had already moved on to Phoenix:

> Dear Frank,
>
> The grapevine has it that you have effected your "Escape from the Gulag" (soon to be a major motion picture). Congratulations, and welcome back to civilization, at least insofar as it is practiced in Denver.
>
> In future years you may reflect back on what you learned there [at Chaco]. You shouldn't. The gulag teaches humility and patience. Only those qualities; nothing else. You may notice a slight increase in your drinking capacity, but that will be only temporary.
>
> It was nice to see you in Phoenix with Raymundo and the Rogue Ranger. Come back anytime. I'll be here a while.
>
> Regards,
> Randy

I spent one winter in Chaco, three years ago. Memories of that time still call up strong memories in me, for I loved the emptiness and eerie beauty of the canyon in winter, when the sun burns white in the morning sky and the mesas ignite at sunset and coyotes leave tracks in the snow by your bedroom window at night. But it got to me finally, sometime in late February, when I began to stagger through my days like a punch-drunk boxer. I wouldn't have survived with my sanity intact if I hadn't had a friend there and if we hadn't observed, every Tuesday night, a pagan ritual of our own invention.

Randy didn't want to be in the canyon that winter. He had accepted the archeologist's job the previous May because it was a promotion, but his wife and two daughters had stayed behind in Albuquerque, where the family had been living, and it was to Albuquerque that Randy fled every weekend. (Friday mornings he would begin to study the sky carefully, trying visually to stall bad weather. It worked. In the three years he was at Chaco, he never failed to get out.) He would leave for town at 5:05 Friday afternoon and return just in time for work Monday morning. Tuesday nights, though, were reserved, religiously, for chess and whiskey.

I would show up at his door after dinner, already long after dark, and we would begin playing and drinking to the sound of "The Home of Happy Feet" on New Mexico Public Radio. Usually we would get in three games, each a bit more ragged than the last, before our concentration gave out. Then we would sit talking quietly while we listened to Randy's old, scratchy Joan Baez recordings. Those were lovely, melancholy evenings, for Randy had reached the vantage point of middle age from which he could discern the course and probable destination of his own life and from which he enjoyed commenting wryly on mine. We would talk about how we had ended up in Chaco and about what that choice signified for us and for others in the canyon. Life, or maybe I should say people's lives, fascinated Randy. He was convinced that the canyon attracted people who were hiding from something in the "outside world" and who thought the canyon would shield them, people who were exhibiting what he liked to call "avoidance behavior."

"Crutcher," he would say to me, addressing me by my middle name, "get your ass out of here."

Eventually we would lapse into comfortable silence, listening to Baez's plaintive voice ("Sad-eyed lady, should I wait?"), enjoying each other's quiet company. Then, sometime after midnight, I would stagger to my feet, bundle up, and step into the gelid darkness. Randy would accompany me outside in order to pee from the edge of his front porch, a personal ritual he loved dearly. I would stand for a minute in his driveway before saying good night, admiring the magnificent winter sky and the ice-encrusted, starlit landscape, shivering as the chill began to invade my body, and feeling again—sharply, in my chest—the approach of that awful sense of solitude and desolation that only a winter in Chaco Canyon can produce.

Yes, winters are tough, but even then we are not as alone as we feel. Out of sight all around us, as if waiting silently offstage, are the Navajos, many of them still living in dirt-floored hogans and cinder-block houses without electricity or running water. Some work on the park's maintenance crew, but most in this area survive by getting temporary jobs on the highway or in Farmington, by herding sheep, goats, and cattle, or by selling their jewelry and rugs to tourists and traders. They are by nature a reserved people, and hard to get to know. After working here for five years, I can count only a handful as good friends. It is not just me. To outsiders in general they present a facade of indifference as unnerving as it is frustrating. Driving home from Farmington, I sometimes pass Navajo trucks on Route 44, the parents and grandma in the cab, the kids in the bed. When I make eye contact with the kids, they sometimes nod, but they never smile or wave. Even the young ones, six or seven years old, appear solemn and unyielding.

The Navajos seem a part of this landscape, but the archeologists assure me that they are relative latecomers, that their ancestors, a nomadic people out of northern Canada, didn't arrive in the Four Corners area until after the Anasazi had abandoned the pueblos in Chaco Canyon. I like to imagine those people—the nomads, the first Navajos—coming into this area: in small bands probably, on foot, dragging travois, tired from months or years of travel and skirmish; and I like to imagine them surveying its empty spaces for the first time, excited by the prospect of what they see, sensing its promise. Their journey ended here, on the high desert plateau; this place became the home they had been seeking. They began to tell stories of their emergence from the earth at a mesa called Dzilth-na-o-dith-hle, just north of Chaco, and to think of their homeland, outside of which most Navajos still feel uncomfortable, as an area demarcated by four sacred mountains on the edges of the desert. From their Puebloan neighbors, whom they sometimes raided for food and women, they learned to weave and later to make jewelry, crafts that we today consider distinctively Navajoan.

▼ Chaco Canyon ▼

I often wonder what the early Navajos thought of the abandoned pueblos, the ghost towns, they found in the canyon. Apparently they regarded them with suspicion from the beginning, because they didn't move into them, didn't settle anywhere near them in fact. Even today, because of their strong beliefs about the dead, most Navajos keep their distance from the ruins. In the traditional Navajo world view a dying person's spirit journeys to a subterranean afterworld inhabited by powerful, dangerous beings called *ch'inde*. The *ch'inde* can return to the earth's surface to harm the living, and an individual's *ch'inde* often returns to the place where the person died. There, like a deadly microbe, it waits to infect those who disturb it. Such death-places must be avoided. When someone dies in a hogan, for example, traditional Navajos knock out the north wall of the structure (marking it as a death-house), bury the body nearby, and abandon the place. And they don't go back.

For that reason the local Navajos rarely visit the Anasazi ruins, which they know contain human burials, and most view the canyon itself, with its concentration of ruins, as a malevolent place. People spend time in the ruins only if they are ignorant of the danger or if they are trying to gain the power of the *ch'inde*; that is, if they are witches. Traditional Navajos believe that evil-minded people in this world often succumb to the temptation to use supernatural powers for their own nefarious purposes —to wreak vengeance on their enemies, say, or to gain personal wealth. Accidents, sudden illness, unexplained death—all may be signs of witchcraft, whose practitioners are also said to indulge in incest and necrophilia—

the dark, erotic underbelly of human experience. To perform their evil magic, witches roam the world under cover of darkness, robbing graves for corpse poison to grind into powder (which they trick their victims into inhaling or ingesting) and transforming themselves into were-animals (usually wolves or coyotes) to travel great distances. Out in places like Chaco Canyon strange things happen in the middle of the night, things that can rouse you uneasily out of deep sleep, things that can hurt you. You take precautions. A Navajo friend of mine carries a bag of sacred corn pollen with her to ward off the effects of witchcraft, and a couple of years ago she and her husband hired a medicine man to cure her of mysterious fits of crying that they believed were the result of a witching. For traditional Navajos the world is not benign, and illness and misfortune are never accidental. When something bad happens, someone has caused it.

Of course, the local Navajos regard those of us who live in the canyon by choice with a great deal of suspicion, feelings reinforced by what history has taught them about our race. For many Indians, white people are, quite simply, embodiments of evil. In her novel *Ceremony* Leslie Marmon Silko (herself a Pueblo of Laguna Indian) has a Navajo medicine man tell the story of how white people were created by Indian witchcraft. The story recounts a gathering of witches a long time ago in the *malpais*, the lava-rock badlands, near Mount Taylor, a prominent peak southeast of Chaco.

The gathering soon turns into a contest of dark powers, some of the witches showing off the evil objects in their secret bundles and others the gruesome contents of their cooking pots ("dead babies simmering in blood / circles of skull cut away / all the brains sucked out"). Finally only one is left. This last witch doesn't try to compete with the others. This one simply tells a story, a story that will begin to happen, the witch says, with the telling. At first the others laugh, but the story soon quiets them. It describes the coming of a white-skinned people who see the world only as a dead thing, an object; a people who will bring with them war and starvation and disease. ("Entire tribes will die out / covered with festered sores / shitting blood / vomiting blood.") It tells of how those people, in their madness, finally will destroy the world. The other witches become uneasy. The story frightens them, and they ask this witch to call it back. But of course it is too late. The events foretold are already happening.

It is a sad coincidence of history that what most Navajos dread in this canyon—the Anasazi ruins—is what has always drawn whites here, despite the presence of the Navajos. Since a U.S. Army expedition first mapped the ruins in 1849, the Navajos have been subjected to a steadily increasing number of whites—explorers and homesteaders first, then archeologists, finally the park's employees and visitors. Most of those people have coped with the Navajos by avoiding or ignoring them. In recent years, however, the Park Service has made a deliberate effort to garner the good will of the local community, allowing Navajo families, for example, to haul drinking water from the park's deep-water well. Despite such gestures, relations between the park and the locals remain strained. The situation has been aggravated in recent years by Chaco's ascending reputation in the archeological world and by its prominence in the media, which have acted to bring record numbers of visitors to the park and to attract funds for a long-planned, though ill-conceived, park improvement program.

Since the late 1960s the park's management plan has called for closing the present entrance road at the north boundary and diverting traffic onto another existing road—one with signs designating it a county highway—that runs eastward roughly parallel to the north rim of the canyon, drops into a tributary drainage of the Chaco, and eventually intersects an existing service road in the park. Using the new approach, visitors would need to check in at the park's visitor center before seeing the ruins, a desirable restriction impossible to enforce under the present arrangement.

Several years ago, during the initial work on a paved loop road in the park, the contractor began hauling fill sand and other material over the new route. A Navajo man named Kee Tso Yazzie, whose land the road crosses, promptly barricaded it with an old truck frame and axles, a sofa, and assorted other junk. When the contractor cleared the road, Yazzie barricaded it again, dug trenches across it, and, during a confrontation at the barricade with the federal highway project engineer, pulled a rifle and ordered the man off his property. At that point the park's superintendent invited Yazzie to the visitor center to talk about the dispute.

Through an interpreter—for he doesn't speak English, or at least pretends not to when it suits him—Yazzie demanded to know why he hadn't been told about the new road. He said that he didn't want the park's traffic passing by his house and across his land. The superintendent explained that the road was a public road and that Yazzie had damned well better accept that fact. Yazzie responded in kind, and the meeting ended abruptly. The superintendent then contacted the Department of the Interior field solicitor in Santa Fe to initiate legal action against Yazzie. (During that furor over the road an owl feather, sign of a witching, was found under the accelerator pedal of a government truck parked overnight in front of the chief ranger's house. I recall asking Franklin later that day what the feather meant. "It doesn't mean anything," he snapped. "I don't believe in that superstition. . . . Where did you find it?" I told him. "Well," he said with grim satisfaction, "he deserved it anyway.")

There was a problem: Despite the county signs the road that crosses Kee Tso Yazzie's land is not a public road. It crosses his land, and that of other Navajos in the area, without benefit of a public right-of-way, a fact that had gone undetected by the people who had prepared the park's management plan years before. From a legal point of view Yazzie had been allowing other people to use the road only out of neighborliness, and unless the Park Service was willing to initiate condemnation proceedings—a tricky matter on Indian land—it had no way to force him to open the road. Yazzie had the park buffaloed. That year's work would be seriously delayed if the contractor couldn't use the new route. Yazzie, however, was willing to negotiate, at least that time, and an agreement was signed whereby the contractor obtained a right-of-way for six months. But when the agreement lapsed, Yazzie promptly closed the road again, and it remains closed to this day. No one knows if the park will ever get its new approach.

Opinion is divided in the Navajo community over Kee Tso Yazzie and what he is doing. Some Navajos dislike him for his inveterate orneriness, but most of his neighbors, including Franklin and one of the park's other full-time maintenance men, both of whom also live along the road, quietly support him.

I have met Yazzie. One day I drove out toward his house to relay a message to him, given to me by some visitors, that his brother-in-law's truck had broken down on the road to Crownpoint, south of the canyon. Since I didn't know exactly where he lived and, more important, how he would receive me, I went first to Franklin's house, hoping to persuade him to deliver the message for me.

"He lives right back there on the hill. Why don't you deliver it yourself?" Franklin asked with a fiendish grin. "Afraid he'll scalp you?"

I said I was more worried he'd shoot me.

"Then give it to Ben Wilson. He's Kee Tso's brother-in-law too."

I gave the message to Wilson. Then, as I was driving toward the park, Yazzie himself sped up behind me and flashed his headlights on and off. I stopped in the road, and he pulled up on my right, so that I had to lean across the front seat to talk to him through the passenger-side window.

"Heard you were lookin' for me," he said, as in a movie showdown.

I told him I was and repeated the message, wondering how he had found out so quickly and suddenly aware that his left hand, out of sight, probably was fingering a gun.

"Is that all you wanted?"

I nodded. I had glimpsed him briefly in the visitor center the year before; now I studied him in fascination. He is an unusual-looking Navajo, with a shock of coarse gray hair, a long, ragged gray beard, and what I am tempted to call Jimmy Blacksmith eyes: large, dark, energized, unblinking. Someone had told me that he reads the Bible avidly and is a self-proclaimed preacher, and, yes, I could see a kind of messianic fervor in those eyes.

He asked me again if that was all I wanted, and I assured him it was. He stared straight at me for a minute—unusual for a Navajo—appraising me and my story. Finally he seemed satisfied.

"Thank you, thank you very much," he said, relaxing visibly. Then, in clear, staccato English, he delivered a short sermon: He told me that we shouldn't change the road and especially shouldn't pave it, that a paved road would just mean "more people and more trouble," that we already had enough. He asked me how long I had worked at the park, and I told him. He nodded, still staring straight at me but squinting now, looking through me. "Tell them not to pave the road," he said again, with finality. And then he was backing up and turning around and heading home.

Kee Tso Yazzie has good reasons for not wanting a paved road near his house. He is worried about his children and livestock, about unwanted visitors, about vandalism and theft. But I'm not sure that those legitimate concerns explain his behavior or account for his fervor. There is, I suspect, more at work here: a century of defeat, neglect, and bitterness, and the determination of a people to survive.

Lurking somewhere behind those eyes, animating them, are stories (heard as a child and repeated to his children) of Kit Carson and his soldiers slaughtering livestock and burning fields and orchards and starving the People out of Canyon de Chelly; of the Long Walk to Fort Sumner in eastern New Mexico; of years of disease, starvation, and helplessness; of being allowed finally to return home to the area south of Dzilth-na-o-dith-hle; of BIA regulations and legal rights-of-way and encroachments by white homesteaders, white archeologists, white tourists. Yazzie is only doing what any Navajo, given the opportunity, would do. A friend of mine on the reservation says, "They'll stick it to you every chance they get. They're repaying you." It has become their second nature.

I often work with the Navajos in the park. They are taciturn, watchful men, and when two or more of them are with me, they speak together in Navajo, not bothering to interpret.

Although the local Navajos tend to avoid the ruins and canyon, many have spent their entire lives in the surrounding area, and this place—the sagebrush desert of the high plateau—is the only home they have known. I often wonder how they perceive this landscape, so familiar to them, so much a part of their lives. Is it beautiful in their eyes and minds? Do they dream about it when they are away?

By the same token, I sometimes wonder what our visitors think as they journey to the canyon for the first time. After arriving, some of them ask me (with a laugh) what I did to deserve such a terrible assignment, and as one who once stood in their shoes, I think I can appreciate their sentiments. The road to Chaco is, after all, long and rough, and the canyon itself is not a spectacular cleft in the earth like de Chelly or Tsegi, but a wide, shallow trough—sun-bleached, sandy, utterly dry. It is a landscape that doesn't appeal naturally to many people. One whose beauty resides in its very desolation: in barren sandstone cliffs, in space and light, in empty vistas and a hemisphere of sky.

Its one extraordinary topographic feature—and the one that sooner or later draws the attention of everyone who comes here—is Fajada Butte, a roughly circular chunk of sandstone detached by erosion from the canyon's south wall, an island of rock floating in an ocean of space. Fajada is not a pinnacle or spire like the ones in Monument Valley, but a squat mass, from some angles appearing nearly as wide as it is high—a pale fortress by day, a black dreadnought on starry nights. Its cliffs appear insurmountable, but if you are determined enough, you can wedge your way up a narrow chimney on its southwest side and follow an exposed trail around and up to its flat summit.

In many stories told by the local Navajos, the butte figures as a vaguely sinister place. According to the one I've heard most often, a female witch lives near the top, luring young men up only to imprison them and starve them to death. Only stories perhaps, but I've never felt comfortable making the climb. (I also recall that years ago, as a graduate student in archeology, Randy excavated a site at the base of the butte that contained the skeletons of a man, woman, and child—all, in his opinion, murdered.) Nevertheless, I can't deny that I too feel the power this landmark exerts on our visitors. Often I feel my eye being drawn in its direction, and its image seems always to hover on the periphery of my thoughts about the canyon.

Although the butte is the canyon's most prominent landmark and, in some sense, its symbol, most people travel here, at least initially, to view the prehistoric ruins. In the early 1970s an archeological survey crew counted more than 2,200 sites within the park's boundaries. The most impressive of those, and the ones that have always garnered the most attention, are the great houses of Chaco, ten of which are concentrated along the canyon's lower reach. The largest of the great houses, and the one that occupies a central position in the complex, is Pueblo Bonito. When it was occupied, Bonito contained nearly eight hundred rooms terraced around a semicircular plaza, and its outer wall rose to five stories. The stone masonry here was the finest in the prehistoric

Southwest. The Anasazi lavished care on their creation, devoting countless hours of labor to quarrying, shaping, carrying, and laying the sandstone blocks.

It housed their treasures as well. During excavation the site yielded an astonishing quantity of artifacts: fifty thousand pieces of turquoise, hundreds of ceramic pots, dozens of macaw and parrot skeletons (the live birds obtained in trade from ancient Mesoamerica, probably because the Anasazi prized their bright feathers for use in ceremonies), carved and painted wooden flutes four feet in length . . . A thousand years ago Bonito was a place of great wealth and status within the Anasazi world. No one knows, though, exactly who lived here. The religious or political leaders? A class of merchants? Of artisans? Almost a hundred human skeletons were dug out of rooms in the ruin, some with impressive offerings of turquoise and pottery, but the identity of those people remains unknown.

During the summers we give guided tours of Bonito every afternoon, but visitors are also free to wander through the ruin on their own, following a graveled walk around its outer wall and through its intricate room block. At the northwest corner of the ruin, however, a sandy, unmarked path cuts west along the base of the canyon's north cliff. Several hundred yards down this path a barbed-wire fence encloses a small cemetery overgrown with grasses and weeds. Low mounds of rocks mark the graves of about fifteen Navajos who lived and died near the canyon in the early years of this century; only one is identified by a small headstone. In the middle of the cemetery, surrounded by the Navajo graves, stands a large headstone with a bronze plaque bolted to it and, leaning against it, a second slab of sandstone—the original marker—still inscribed clearly, "Richard Wetherell [*sic*] / Died June 22, 1910."

Richard Wetherill is a pioneer figure in this part of the world; a man famous or infamous, as most pioneers are; a man of legendary stature. He was the first to excavate the ruins in Chaco Canyon; the first white man to live here; the first to die. If the Anasazi established the pattern of life in the canyon, of life in extremis, Wetherill established the pattern of relations between the whites and the Indians. His story haunts us to this day, refuses to let us go. It is a curse. The Navajos still mention his name, sometimes pretending they don't know exactly who he was, and the great-grandson of the man who killed him works on the park's maintenance crew today.

Because Wetherill is an important historic figure, a man well-known even in his own era, we should know more about him than we do. While we can trace the course of his life in some detail, however, the man himself remains a shadowy presence, his personality described in contradictory ways by different people who knew him, his motives largely lost to us today. He could read and write—and in fact did write numerous letters to his business contacts and sponsors—but he never took the time to record what he probably considered unimportant personal information. Several years ago I prepared an interpretive talk on Wetherill. I read the family-approved biography, and I read the book that presents the Indians' view of the man. I talked to his great-granddaughter in Santa Fe, and I talked to my Navajo friends in the park, whose great-grandparents were his neighbors and antagonists. I did my research, and I emerged with no clearer image of the man than I had when I started. From our vantage point in history he defies characterization. So, it seems, we must be content with what we know, with the outline of a life.

Wetherill didn't grow up near Chaco or even in New Mexico. He was born in 1858 in Pennsylvania, the oldest of five boys in a Quaker family. His father was struck with wanderlust, though, and the family moved steadily west, finally homesteading a ranch near Mancos, Colorado, in 1880. The Wetherills apparently came to be on good terms with the neighboring Ute Indians, because the Utes permitted them to run their cattle on nearby Mesa Verde. There, chasing strays one snowy December day in 1888, Richard "discovered"—became the first white man to see—the Anasazi cliff dwellings for which the area is famous (an event celebrated by Willa Cather in "The Tom Outland Story" in *The Professor's House*). Although he had no formal training in archeology, he was fascinated by the ruins and he soon gave up his life as a cowboy to devote himself to the discovery and exploration of other archeological sites in the Four Corners area. During his travels he began to hear stories of the great ruins in a remote, desolate canyon in Navajo country to the south, said to be larger than any he had yet seen. The way was long and difficult, though, even for a man like Wetherill, and he didn't make it to Chaco until the fall of 1895. No one knows what his initial reaction to the place was, but he stayed a month that first visit, and by the time he left, he was so taken with the canyon that he had decided to concentrate his energies here. He returned the following summer to set up camp and begin full-time excavations.

During his four summers of work in the canyon, Wetherill oversaw the excavation of about a third of Pueblo Bonito. His work was funded by two wealthy brothers from New York who also hired a young archeologist from Harvard named George Pepper to lend professional expertise. Although Wetherill and Pepper disliked each other intensely (their bitter feud calling to mind more recent ones), work progressed quickly, with the bulk of their collections being shipped to the American Museum of Natural History in New York City, where it remains to this day, and the rest being sold by Wetherill to help finance the project. Their crew consisted of a couple of white shippers and about a dozen local Navajos, men willing to work in the ruin, despite the *ch'inde*, as long as they could periodically hold traditional curing ceremonies, called sings, to decontaminate themselves. (Even today our Navajo ruins stabilization crew takes protective measures. Those who are Christian pray a great deal, and the remainder perform variations of the old sings.) Wetherill and Pepper's original camp abutted the back wall of Bonito, some of whose intact rooms they used for storage. Wetherill also rented one of those rooms to the sporadic visitors who made their way to the canyon. I often show that room to interested tourists today, its walls still smoke-blackened from poorly vented fires and a stovepipe poking through the hole that Wetherill knocked in the prehistoric masonry.

Wetherill may not have been a writer or journal-keeper, but he was a self-taught photographer, and a good one. He took hundreds of pictures of the excavations-in-progress and of life-after-work in Chaco Canyon before the turn of the century. The negatives of those photographs are in New York City, but the park has prints of most of them, including a few in which Wetherill himself appears. I've spent several hours studying those particular ones, looking for clues. He was not an especially handsome man: a broad, somewhat doughy face; a thick, drooping mustache in the style of the times; deep wrinkles around his eyes. Perhaps what strikes me most about the pictures is that he never smiles. Always he appears tight-lipped, laconic, sullen. A tough man to deal with.

Although Wetherill is well-known for his archeological work, his other ventures in the canyon were equally significant. In 1900, in order to gain legal ownership of the ruins and prevent other archeologists from preempting his discovery, he filed a homestead application for land on which Bonito and two of its neighboring great houses are located. By that time he had already constructed a ranch house next to Bonito, using timbers and sandstone blocks scavenged out of the ruin itself. With his sponsors' encouragement and support he had also begun to trade with the Indians, selling supplies and buying Navajo blankets for markets back East. And he had become fluent in Navajo, a tonal language notoriously difficult to master.

Nevertheless, Wetherill's relations with the Indians, like ours with them today, were strained. When I ask the Navajos who work in the park what they have heard about Wetherill and what they think of him, they usually shrug and look away. Usually. "That man Wetherill," Franklin said to me once, "got what he deserved." (Meaning something quite different, Randy once characterized Wetherill as "a man who was always looking for his just deserts.") How much Wetherill brought on himself is difficult to say. Certainly he was capable at times of grievous cruelty. On at least one occasion he locked a Navajo laborer, whom he suspected of stealing artifacts, overnight in his Bonito motel room with a collection of Anasazi skulls. And like us today, he was regarded warily by most of the locals because of his fascination with the ruins. In fact, they began to call him the same thing they called the previous inhabitants of the area: *Anasazi*—loosely translated, "ancient enemy."

By the turn of the century, however, Wetherill's position in the canyon seemed secure. His ranch and trading post were well established, and his excavations were producing large, well-publicized collections. He had claimed a place for himself here, and, for a time at least, the future must have looked promising. Then, in 1900, a number of prominent archeologists in Santa Fe, probably motivated by a combination of professional jealousy and genuine professional concern, began to agitate for legal action against Wetherill. In a series of letters to the secretary of the interior, they alleged that Chaco Canyon was being despoiled "by parties in search of relics for commercial purposes." In response to their allegations the commissioner of the General Land Office ordered Wetherill to halt his excavations until a federal agent could investigate the charges. That man visited Chaco the following year and, although impressed by the quality of the field work, filed a report recommending that the ruins be protected through the establishment of a national park. As a result of that report the cease-and-desist order remained in effect until 1907, when Teddy Roosevelt used his authority under the recently enacted Antiquities Act to proclaim Chaco Canyon a national monument. The federal government subsequently asked Wetherill to relinquish his claim to the land containing the ruins, and he complied. Nevertheless, he retained control over the rest of his ranch and chose to remain in the canyon.

I often wonder why he stayed. After the turn of the century life in Chaco would have been difficult and frustrating for him. Although there is evidence he continued to dig in the ruins and even to sell artifacts, he could no longer do so legally, and his sponsors soon withdrew their financial support. Except for a couple of hired ranch hands, he and his family—his wife and their five young children—found themselves isolated in the middle of Navajo country. The nearest supplies were at the railroad stop in Thoreau, a two-day wagon ride to the south. There was no telephone, no radio. The winters would have been long and hard. I don't know why he stayed . . . Maybe the canyon wouldn't let him go. Maybe it held him the same way it held the Anasazi, and still holds the Navajos, and those of us who are drawn here despite what this place does to us. I don't know why he stayed. He should have broken free.

Wetherill's last years were difficult and unhappy. He struggled to make a living on his ranch, increasing his herds of horses and sheep and gradually usurping land north of the canyon which neither he nor the Indians owned, but on which the Navajos had traditionally grazed their livestock. Several times he tried to fence them off that land, and each time he was ordered by the local Indian agent to take down his fences. The Indians also complained that Wetherill granted them credit at his trading post, then without notice appropriated their livestock as payment. The already tense situation was aggravated when Wetherill hired as his ranch foreman a bad-tempered gunman out of Texas named Bill Finn.

On June 22, 1910, Wetherill and Finn returned to the canyon from a cattle drive to Gallup to discover that a Navajo from the nearby community of Lake Valley had "stolen"—repossessed—a horse of disputed ownership while they had been away. Wetherill sent Finn to retrieve the animal. Finn rode to Lake Valley, found the Navajo, pistol-whipped him into unconsciousness, and brought the horse back to the canyon. The Navajo's brother-in-law came home shortly thereafter and found his sister crying over what she thought was her dead husband. She told her brother who had done it, and he rode toward the canyon to settle the matter with Wetherill, stopping to buy bullets at a trading post along the way. As he approached Pueblo Bonito, he encountered Wetherill and Finn on horseback, driving cattle down-canyon.

From that point the details of the story are mud-
dled. According to Finn, the Navajo ambushed them.
According to Navajo witnesses, whom I am inclined to
believe, the two white men saw the Indian, recognized
him, and, drawing their pistols and shouting threats, galloped toward him. He quickly dismounted, pulled his rifle
from its scabbard, aimed, and fired, hitting Wetherill in the
chest. Finn promptly turned and galloped back toward the
ranch house, leaving his boss bleeding to death on the
ground. According to the testimony of the Navajo himself,
he then walked over to Wetherill, who at that time may or
may not have been alive, asked him, "Are you still on the
warpath, Anasazi?" and shot him through the head.

Wetherill's ranch house and outbuildings stood
until the 1950s, when the Park Service decided—in hind-
sight, regrettably—to demolish them. By that time they
had fallen into a state of disrepair, and funds weren't
available for restoration and maintenance. Wetherill's reputation as an archeologist also had declined (before being
rehabilitated in the 1960s and later), and the Park Service, rightly or wrongly, was trying to downplay his presence in the canyon. Some Park Service managers also
espoused the view that the presence of the historic structures "contaminated" the prehistoric ruins and landscape
in the vicinity of Bonito. The last of Wetherill's outbuildings, a stone wagon shed, was dismantled in 1958.

Although the structures are gone, you can still find
scattered debris where they stood—shards of glass and
glazed pottery, pieces of baling wire, a window pulley
frozen by rust. During my time here I have explored most

of the country within the park's boundaries, and occasionally I come across other reminders of this man and his era:
an inscription he carved in 1909 on a sandstone plug near
the summit of Fajada Butte; an old mine shaft up one of
the side canyons where he dug coal for the winter; a drawing that someone, probably a Navajo, scratched on a boulder, showing a man in a cowboy hat on a horse being shot
by another man, the bullets arcing across the sandstone to
his chest and head. There is more here, of course, than just
those reminders of Wetherill's life and times. As I wander
through the canyon, I also come across scatters of Anasazi
potsherds, old hogan rings, and cliff walls decorated with
rock art. In its sandy soil and rocky crevices the canyon
holds the accumulated debris of all of its people.

The longer I am here, the more I am fascinated
by those who have preceded me. Often these days I find
myself thinking about the Anasazi, the ones who settled
here first. Who were they and what did they see in the
canyon? As they stood on the mesas looking down into
it, what images were playing in their minds? I look and
wonder, because if Chaco is distinguished by anything, it
is distinguished by its utter lack of resources. One of the
ironies of Chacoan archeology is that most of the artifacts that we consider distinctive of their culture were
produced from exotic materials. The chert and obsidian
for their points and arrowheads, the temper for their pottery, the turquoise for their jewelry—all had to be
imported. Even the large roof timbers for their pueblos
probably were cut in distant mountains and carried on
their backs to the canyon.

▼ Chaco Canyon ▼

But the most serious problem for the Anasazi would have been water. As I explore the canyon today, I search for water more than anything else. I look for it in the likely places: near cottonwood trees in the arroyos, in potholes in the slickrock, under shady overhangs at the heads of the side canyons. I don't find much, because there isn't much here. In fact, I know of only three seeps in the entire park, basin-sized pools whose shores are always crowded with the prints of thirsty wildlife. I've been told you can dig six or eight feet in the arroyo and hit brackish water, but I doubt anyone could drink it. And the wash itself, the Rio Chaco, flows for only a few hours or days after heavy rains and snows. Puddles and potholes hold water longer, but it soon turns fetid and unpalatable.

Everyone who comes to the canyon, whether to live or visit, must cope with its terrible aridity. Before they had pickup trucks and fifty-five-gallon drums, the Navajos carefully maintained the seeps in the area. And until he dug a shallow well in the arroyo, Wetherill hauled all of his drinking water in horse-drawn wagons. The park drilled a three-thousand-foot-deep well in 1972, but we still have problems with our supply. Every summer that I've worked here, one of our water lines has burst or the treatment plant has broken down, leaving us dry for a day or two or three. I've learned to keep five gallons of drinking water under my kitchen sink for such emergencies. Even our visitors may be affected, and we try to educate them to the value of water and the dangers of not having enough. We ask them to conserve in the campground, and we tell them to carry a gallon in their cars in case of breakdown.

Like us today, the Anasazi a thousand years ago had to contend with the problem of water. The archeologists tell me that the canyon was getting the same precipitation then as it does now, about nine inches a year, most of it in the form of summer thundershowers. Hardy and careful though the Anasazi must have been, how did they survive? The most likely answer is, alas, the most mundane: that the water table was higher then and that small springs along the bases of the cliffs, long since dried up, supplied them with dependable drinking water. The canyon floor today is littered with thousands of potsherds; many of those vessels probably were ollas and ceramic canteens, dropped and broken during the transport of water.

Even if springs provided their drinking water, however, the Anasazi would have needed to utilize runoff efficiently. Thus one finds in the side canyons the remains of masonry dams they built to impound water pouring off the mesas after heavy rains, water they could have used to wash and shower, to irrigate their fields in the canyon bottom, and to mix the clay-and-sand mortar and plaster for their village walls. And they could have stored some of that water in lidded pots, allowing the silt to settle before drinking it. They still couldn't control the arrival of the rains, though, and for that reason they would have worried about water constantly, prayed for it, dreamed about it. Water would have haunted them, as it haunts their descendants even today.

▼ Chaco Canyon ▼

Pueblo Indians in New Mexico and Arizona still direct their most fervent prayers to the sacred kachinas, the rain-power beings who reside on the mountains surrounding their desert homes. Every year the kachinas must be summoned to bring the vital summer rains, and every year they must be thanked properly for coming. Even today, with electricity to pump water and pickup trucks to haul it, Pueblo Indians consider water a sacred gift.

The question of water, like water itself, percolates quietly through my thoughts about the canyon. If Chaco was, even a thousand years ago, a dry canyon in the middle of a still drier expanse of sagebrush desert, why did the Anasazi settle and flourish here? After all, the San Juan River, one of the major water sources in the Southwest, flows forty miles north, through an area the Chacoans ostensibly controlled. Why, then, didn't their center develop along its banks, where life would have been comparatively easy? What was special about the canyon? I ask the archeologists, and they respond with theories that purport to explain the Anasazis' presence here rationally. The canyon was easily defended, they say, or it was centrally located in the San Juan Basin. Or, most ingeniously, the very poverty of the environment necessitated the cooperation of large numbers of people.

I nod as they talk. Their theories sound plausible, convincing even. But later, looking around the canyon, I wonder again, and I remember what I have always known: that there is no good reason for people to live here. Perhaps, then, the answer lies elsewhere—not in physical setting, geographic location, or economics—but in the hearts and minds of the Anasazi themselves. And perhaps it isn't rational, doesn't make sense. Perhaps those people flourished in Chaco because they believed, as the Hopis today believe of the barren mesas they inhabit in Arizona, that the canyon was their spiritual home, the place they were destined to be.

Just as no one knows why they were here, so no one knows what happened to them. Maybe we shouldn't be surprised that they finally gave up and left, that the canyon wore them down in the end, as it seems to wear down everyone who is drawn here. Still, I can't help wondering what finally went wrong, what caused them to give up after enduring for so long. There is no evidence of warfare, little of strife. Disease—an epidemic—is another possibility, but, again, little evidence supports such a theory. (I find myself wondering sometimes if they too suffered dehydrated brains and related maladies.)

The most plausible explanation is that their water supply finally became too undependable and that food shortages, brought on by the depletion of the soil and aggravated by a mild but persistent drought, caused their social fabric to fray and eventually to tear. The end in Chaco may not have been violent, but it probably wasn't pleasant either. In the end, with their crops withering in the fields and their children crying for food, the people may have come to believe that this canyon, their home for so long, was a cursed spot, a place from which their prayers could not escape. And perhaps what happened here a thousand years ago explains why few of the modern Pueblos claim Chaco as their ancestral home and why we seldom have Indian visitors today.

I wish I could tell you more. I wish I could give you answers. I can't. The Anasazi didn't record what was happening in the canyon a thousand years ago, at least not in any form we can translate. The canyon's walls are covered with the sometimes fantastic, often grotesque figures and geometric designs they pecked and carved into the varnished sandstone, but there is no Rosetta stone, nothing to tell us what the images mean, if indeed they ever "meant" anything.

The most common motif in the canyon is a spiral petroglyph, traveling inward either clockwise or counterclockwise. The archeological survey crew found hundreds of those spirals scattered along the walls of the canyon, some in panels with other petroglyphs, some by themselves. Often as I walk, my eye is drawn to the cliff by the familiar concentric design, and often as I look, I wonder what significance the spiral held for the Anasazi. Why this particular design? Why so often? On the Hopi mesas tribal elders inscribe spiral petroglyphs to symbolize the migrations of the various Hopi clans in their search for the center of the universe. The spiral seems an appropriate design, drawing the eye into its center much as the Hopis claim to have been drawn to their mesas in Arizona. As the Anasazi, perhaps, were drawn to Chaco Canyon. A vortex, with the canyon at its center. The interpretation is tempting, but even if it is correct, we still don't have the answer, still don't know what was going on inside the heads of the Anasazi as they pecked and carved those images into the cliffs, still don't know what stories they were telling themselves about why this canyon is special.

Our trailers have porches and picnic tables, and on summer evenings I like to sit outside after dark and listen to the sounds of the desert and watch the stars wheel slowly across the sky. Even in June, though, I often wear a sweatshirt, for the nights can yet be chilly. Sometimes I feel a wave of dense, cool air slide off the mesa, and on those nights I know that the temperature will dip below freezing in the hour before dawn. I've been here for six Junes now, and in every one we've had a freeze in the middle of the month.

Six summers and a winter. A trivial length of time by some standards—a heartbeat in the life of the canyon and insubstantial even on a human scale, compared to being born, living one's entire life, and dying in this place, as thousands of Anasazi did. And yet, with the exception of Richard Wetherill and a handful of others, I've lived here longer than any Anglo. The permanent park staff has turned over a couple of times since I first came, and other seasonals rarely return for even a second summer. People have begun to wonder about me, begun to wonder why I'm still here. What do you see in the place? they ask. Why do you come back? The ruins are interesting, but there can't be much to do. They are right, of course, and how can I tell them otherwise?

Sitting at my picnic table, I often hear the demented barking of the coyotes as they roam the darkened canyon. Sometimes a single one is answered by others in the opposite direction: a coyote chorus—inhuman, eerie, maniacal. Like the Navajos, the modern Pueblo Indians view the coyote as a vaguely sinister animal, at best a trickster, at worst an evil presence. I wonder what the Anasazi thought about them? Whenever I hear them calling and answering, I imagine all of the cottontails and jacks in between cowering under their bushes, ears alert, noses twitching, waiting in suppressed frenzy for the sound of padded footsteps and the snarl of canines, the last sounds they will hear.

Two years ago, after a particularly hard summer, I said I was leaving for good. I did leave, in fact, intending never to return. I was tired of driving the road, of dealing with ornery Navajos, of living in this closed, neurotic community. But a funny thing happened. I missed it. Every place else seemed too easy, too lacking in challenge. And the emotional investment—I had so much to lose. My friends were here, and what I took (and still take) to be, for a time, my place in the world. Like others before me, and without my even realizing it, the canyon had become my home. How could I leave when I was just beginning to understand it? How could I go elsewhere?

Last week I was aroused from deep, dream-laden sleep by someone knocking lightly on my door. Four knocks. The curtains were open in the bedroom, and by starlight I made out the face of the clock: 4:30. As I lay in bed, groggy and slow to get up, I recalled other knocks just before the ones that had awakened me—or had I dreamed them?—and suddenly, inexplicably, I felt a vague foreboding. I swung slowly out of bed, picking up the flashlight on the night table instead of turning on the lamp, and made my way to the front door. I squinted through its latticed window before opening it. Nothing. I could sense the cool air waiting beyond the threshold, but something compelled me to step into it anyway. The other trailers were dark and deserted-looking, spectral, and the still air seemed brittle. I was only wearing cotton shorts and a T-shirt, and I began to shiver in the early morning chill. Once I thought I saw headlights swinging around in the maintenance yard, but I closed my eyes to listen for the engine—nothing—and when I opened them again, the headlights were gone.

Maybe someone had knocked on the back door? I went inside and through the living room and out onto the back porch—empty and quiet. I could see the silhouette of Fajada Butte then, and I became aware, for the first time that night, of the vitreous black sky overhead, of the Milky Way floating at zenith, of the crystalline infinitude of stars. I shivered again, unsure of what was happening, unable to move. As I looked at the butte, two stars fell through the sky over it, burning toward its flat summit, dying above its black mass.

Four Corners

W est from Shiprock. The August sun, a distant, megawatt incandescent bulb, rises behind me over Mesa Verde, illuminating these everyday marvels of the Navajo reservation: an old woman sits solemnly in the passenger's seat of a truck, holding a lamb in her lap; a kid wearing a Walkman trots a horse toward a far-off herd of sheep and goats; a man dressed in rodeo finery but for his missing boots walks resolutely along the shoulder of the highway.

West to Rattlesnake, Beclabito, and Teec Nos Pos, and then north toward Cortez five miles. I'm close now. And then a sign and the turnoff. Pay a buck to the woman at the toll booth. Closer. "Slowly," a sign warns. And another: "Movie cameras prohibited unless with proper permit from the Navajo Tribe Film and Media Commission." Finally the end of the road, the parking lot, and, yes, in the middle of the asphalt lot, protected from errant traffic by four galvanized steel guardrails, the object of my quest, the only point in our illustrious nation common to four sovereign states, our own manufactured geographic phenomenon—Four Corners National Monument, U.S.A.

The vendors are already here, most of them anyway, their pickups parked behind the forty tin-roofed vending booths that surround the monument's parking lot, boomtown's little plaza. The adults are setting up their tables and arranging their silver-and-turquoise wares, while their kids wander wide-eyed and waiflike between the booths. The smell of fry bread and corn dogs wafts through the air, reminding me of distant attractions of my youth, Glen Echo and Ocean View. Across the parking lot a Sno-Cone machine revs up.

I sit in the open back of my Datsun station wagon, munching on a fresh corn dog and looking forward to a day on the fringe of the dream, observing the ways of the natives, the ways of the tourists, and the glories of American free enterprise, Navajo style.

9:15 AM. I am amazed by the volume of traffic. At any one time, between twenty and thirty cars are parked rather haphazardly around the perimeter of the unmarked lot, and a few more slowly circle the monument itself. Over in their designated lot, behind the vending booths, by the outhouses, a half-dozen RVs sit in an orderly row, noses to the highway. Exiting their vehicles and dodging the circling traffic, people converge on the monument like lawyers on a gruesome accident. There they mill in confusion around the guardrails while awaiting their turn to step up onto the cement platform, center stage, and take, or have taken, the obligatory vacation photograph.

9:45 AM. I never realized before how many respectable-looking retired couples travel on motorcycles. Not cute little bikes, either, but big muthas, Honda Goldwings mostly, with aerodynamic fairings and fiberglass saddle bags, pulling matching single-axled trailers. The riders' helmets have built-in CB radios and look like the heads of space suits. Most come from the Midwest. Indiana, Ohio. Mom and Pop out discovering America on their pension from GM or Goodyear. Traveling in pairs and threesomes. Smiling and waving to the Navajo vendors as they circle the monument one final time before they head out on the highway, lookin' for adventure.

10:35 AM. A Mercury Marquis with Missouri plates parks across from me. After disembarking from the vacationmobile, Dad leads his charges to the monument. He is jocund and talkative, and dressed for action in bermuda-length cutoff jeans, a white round-neck T-shirt, white over-the-calf socks, and Nike running shoes. And crowned by a sporty green, white, and red driving cap. He lines up Mom and the two kids—a dazed-looking boy about eleven and a bored-looking teen-aged girl—in front of the monument and begins fiddling with his camera and its various lenses.

"Dad, would you hurry up, please," the girl says, embarrassed by the elaborate production and the attention of the onlookers.

"C'mon, Dad," the boy chimes in.

"Just a minute, just a minute. I want a good picture. Let's see, if I use the telephoto lens, those mountains back there will look like they're next door."

"Honest to God, Clyde, would you please just take the picture."

"Just hold your water, Mom. You'll thank me when we're looking at these pictures next month."

As Clyde fiddles intently with his camera, a black woman walks quietly onto the monument behind Mom and the kids, turns, and, as her companion videotapes her, smiles and quickly signs a greeting to the friends back home, her hands fluttering like a dove's wings.

11:15 AM. I decide to take a stretch. First I inspect the monument itself. Up close, I must confess, it disappoints. Elevated four short steps above the parking lot, it consists of a badly cracked cement slab divided into quadrants by crisscrossing diagonal metal strips. Inset in each quadrant is the name of the appropriate state, spelled out in tile against a contrasting tile background—the entire matrix in a state of disintegration—and an oxidized bronze plaque bearing the appropriate state seal. At the midpoint of each guardrail enclosing the monument a sun-bleached state flag droops from its pole like a wilted sunflower.

The monument's tattiness does nothing to dispel a rumor I've heard often, to the effect that the monument was incorrectly surveyed and that the real Four Corners lies somewhere in the surrounding greasewood and tumbleweeds, unmarked and forgotten.

Dismayed but undeterred by my inspection of the monument, I press on to the information center, housed in a large prefab hogan on the west side of the parking lot, along the Arizona-Utah state line. The center sells cards and curios, and its inside walls are decorated with faded posters and maps, dusty Navajo rugs, and a sand painting of the Great Seal of the Navajo Nation.

As I pay for a postcard, I ask the woman behind the counter why only one person is selling in the Colorado sector.

She pauses for an instant before answering. "That corner belongs to the Utes. They charge too much."

I have to know. How much?

"A thousand dollars a year. One year minimum."

And the Navajo Tribe runs the rest of this operation?

She nods. As I process that fact, it suddenly occurs to me that the "nation" in "Four Corners National Monument" refers, somewhat misleadingly, to the Navajo Nation, not the United States. A clever ruse, on the part of the tribe, in its current quest for American greenbacks. Repaying us, so to speak, for past kindnesses.

How much does the Navajo Tribe charge the vendors?

"Two dollars a day."

How does a person get a booth? I ask, curious about the competition for space.

She looks at me suspiciously, her eyes as narrow and shrewd as a banker's. "The chapter representative from Teec handles it. You have to apply to him for a booth, and you gotta be an Indian," she answers firmly.

11:55 AM. Back at the Datsun I eat a Navajo taco—a dense piece of fry bread heaped high with beans, onions, cheese, lettuce, and tomato but lacking in spice—and drink a cold can of Dr Pepper, recently purchased from a vendor in the New Mexico sector. Then, lying down in the back of the station wagon, my feet dangling over the rear bumper, I slip into my customary post-lunch catatonia. I doze for the next hour and a half, occasionally capturing stray dialogue and odd comments from the monument:

Woman, walking toward her car, in a carefree tone: "I think I made it to Colorado, Utah, and . . . What was the other one?"

Man with New York accent, explaining to his kids the financing of the monument: "See, each state probably paid for its own state seal, and the federal government probably paid for the center seal." (Center seal?)

Woman, standing on the monument and looking around in confusion: "Where are the Indian ruins?"

And, perhaps most pointedly, woman, after viewing the monument, in a tone of disappointment and disgust: "Well, let's go see what we can buy."

Finally, rousing myself out of my stupor and sitting up, I am greeted by a vision of sufficiently hallucinogenic quality to make me question the ingredients of my Navajo taco: Two Model A roadsters with California plates cruise into the parking area, circle the monument twice at a good clip—all the while the drivers honking their clownish horns and the passengers waving festively to the vendors and other tourists—and then shoot out of their orbits without so much as slowing down.

1:45 PM. I decide that post-siesta is a good time to tour the monument's commercial district. After a quick trip to the outhouses I head for the vending booths.

▼ Four Corners ▼

At the first few booths I am dazzled by the displays of silver and turquoise jewelry, laid out on the tables like offerings in Pharaoh's tomb, and impressed by the seemingly cut-rate prices. The vendors themselves are friendly in the reserved Navajo way, and small sand paintings on several of the tables advise that those merchants accept traveler's checks, VISA, and MasterCard.

Before long, however, the tables of trinkets begin to blend together. So many necklaces and bracelets. So many rings, earrings, and barrettes. So many alike. My eyes glaze over, my brain shuts down. I begin to walk more quickly and stop less frequently, eager to complete the circuit . . . Until the table in booth seventeen arrests my progress. Displayed on this table is an assortment of beadwork, leatherwork, feathers, and animal parts startlingly different from the usual offerings. I stop and look more closely, wondering about the appeal of this stuff to white tourists. The middle-aged man standing behind the table wears sunglasses, his face dour and forbidding. His portable radio is tuned to AM 660, KTNN, the Voice of the Navajo Nation.

I point to a hairy, clawed hand on one side of the table. Is that a bear paw? I ask.

He watches me from behind his glasses for a minute before answering. "Yeah."

Navajo friends have told me that a few bears still roam the isolated mountains of the reservation. I ask him where he got his paw.

"Colorado," he says without inflection, his face a mask of indifference. He is silent for a few seconds, then surprises me by asking, "Have you ever eaten any bearmeat?"

Knowing that most Navajos consider bears taboo, I tell him no. I find myself staring at this man's face, trying to see his eyes. Have you? I ask before I can stop myself.

He laughs ominously. "Yeah. I was raised on it. Good eatin'. You don't know what you're missin'." He laughs again.

I am a bit unnerved by this bearman but also intrigued by his table of wares. For a minute no one else stops at his booth, and I stand alone inspecting a rattle made of a dried turtle—not just the carapace, but the whole turtle, with its neck and head grotesquely extended, muscles taut, glassy eyes wide open. Finally a kid about ten years old comes up, stares at the table, and carefully picks up a bundle of porcupine quills, tied together with a strip of brain-tanned leather. Without warning the man smacks the kid's hand with a yardstick he's been holding behind his back.

"Look with your eyes, not your hands," he says harshly, sending the kid fleeing.

A minute later he begins to laugh suddenly. I look at him in surprise. What's so funny?

"News report," he says, referring to the Navajo-language broadcast on the radio.

Thinking we might find common ground in humor, I ask him what happened.

"Two Indians drowned yesterday. One in the Rio Grande and one in Morgan Lake," he responds with an evil grin. "I guess they forgot how to swim." He laughs again, heartily, as I begin to edge onward.

2:25 PM. Fortunately, the encounter with the sinister bearman is soon put behind me. Just half a dozen booths later my attention is once again diverted, this time by a display of baseball caps and T-shirts bearing a map of the Four Corners states in a border of stylized Indian design. Always a sucker for exotic headgear, I stop and look.

"Special deal on caps today," the vendor says to me. "Buy four, get the fifth for free."

I laugh and look up. What would I do with five caps? I ask.

"They make great Christmas gifts," she says, smiling. She is a young woman, very pretty, with classic Navajo features framed by long black hair that bleeds to auburn at the tips. Like the bearman, she wears dark glasses, but behind them she looks mysterious, not menacing. Her smile is radiant. I buy a cap. During the course of the transaction I learn that her name is Loretta Tsosie and that she designed the logo on the caps. As we chat—me standing in the August sun, the sky still clear overhead, no thunderstorms today—sweat beads on my forehead.

She notices and asks politely if I'd like to sit in the shade for a while.

Why, yes, thank you. Don't mind if I do.

I spend the next two hours sitting on the ground in Loretta's booth, watching her work and hearing about her life and business.

Although she lives in Shiprock now, Loretta was born in Ogden, Utah. I ask if she's Mormon.

"No," she says matter-of-factly. "I go to the Pentecostal Church in Shiprock."

Knowing that traditional Navajos diligently avoid snakes, believing them to be *ch'inde*—an incarnation of evil spirits—I tell her that Pentecostal Christians in Tennessee, where I once lived, handle snakes in their rapture for the Lord.

"That's disgusting," she responds, restoring my faith in her native credibility.

Loretta has been selling at Four Corners for about five years. She works from March or April until the first heavy snow, six days a week, from early morning until supper time. During the winter she and her sister-in-law, Cheryl, who rents the booth next door, work on their inventory and travel to powwows in Arizona and California. This winter Loretta will drive to the powwows in her new Chevy van, which she purchased recently in Albuquerque.

"Don Biligana at Reliable Chevrolet treated me right and made me a good deal," she says seriously, as if doing a television ad.

In addition to caps and T-shirts Loretta sells beaded key chains, Navajo dolls, and embroidered pillow cases featuring rosy-cheeked Indian boys and girls. But her caps and T-shirts sell the best. I ask her why none of the other vendors has picked up on her sales lead.

Loretta looks at me sternly. "Other people here want to sell shirts and caps, but I won't tell them who my supplier is. If I did, everyone would start selling them and my business would be ruined. One time that man in booth twenty-one followed me to Farmington to see where I went, but I drove to the mall first and lost him."

When people stop to look at her wares, Loretta greets them politely and, as they leave, wishes them a good day. I tell her that she treats strangers nicely.

"Thank you," she answers in a pleased way. "You've got to be nice to people because they're the ones that keep you in business." She pauses for a minute before adding instructively, for my benefit, "You've got to keep the customer satisfied and give him a good deal."

During the two hours I sit with Loretta on this day, which she describes as average, she sells almost seventy dollars worth of merchandise.

What's the strangest thing she's seen at the monument?

She laughs as she remembers. "One time these college kids came in a bus and stood out on the monument and all dropped their pants. Someone took a picture of them, but I never saw it. And another time a group of kids climbed on top of each other and built a . . . Whatta you call it? A pyramid, out on the monument."

I press her for something stranger, something pushing the envelope of bizarre human behavior. For a minute, *nada*. Then she remembers.

"A couple of weeks ago," she says, "some of those Hell's Angels—you know, that motorcycle gang—stopped here."

On their way, I'm guessing, to their annual World Run, which was in Stoner, Colorado, this year. What were they like?

"The men were mostly in their thirties, and they all wore those Harley-Davidson T-shirts. They acted polite, but they were rough-looking. They had beards and tattoos. But those women with them," she says, looking perplexed, "they were pretty. Real pretty. Why . . . Why would a pretty woman want to ride with men like that?"

4:45 PM. Back at the Datsun I sit in the open back nibbling on a Sno-Cone and feeling better about the world.

A family of what I take to be Mennonites has appeared on the monument. The mother and teen-aged daughter wear long dresses and prayer bonnets; the father and son black pants, white shirts, and wide-brimmed black hats. They walk around the monument, inspecting it and conferring quietly with each other. Although they seem interested in this geographic wonder-of-the-world, their expressions are composed and neutral. These are dignified Americans, I find myself thinking, not inclined to the material excesses of our culture. Traveling, perhaps, on some errand of mercy or mutual aid. Would that more of us were like them!

A few minutes later I watch in stunned disbelief as my model Americans climb aboard a yacht-sized RV and motor slowly toward the highway, a sticker on their rear bumper advertising the fact that they, too, have visited Wall Drug, South Dakota.

5:25 PM. Five Navajo kids, elementary-school-aged, appear from behind the booths and, looking around shyly, make their way to the monument. Four scurry onto the monument and assume a pose—two kneeling in front of the other two—while the fifth takes a snapshot. Then the photographer changes places with one of the other kids so that she can be in a picture. The kids are laughing quietly and nudging each other with their shoulders, sharing secrets, speaking in Navajo, those hushed, glottal tones soft in the air.

6:05 PM. Out on the monument the day's activity has slowed. I take advantage of the lull to list the various techniques—some elegant, some not so—of getting one's body into four states at one time: (1) the standard four-point stance, like a football center snapping the ball, with the face craning upward toward the inevitable camera; (2) the modified four-point stance, a.k.a. the frog position or hunker position (this one has the advantage that the person more naturally faces the inevitable camera); (3) large-bottomed people simply sitting on the center point, their flab extending over small parts of four states; (4) lying down, either supine or prone; (5) the arched-back position, belly to the sun, a.k.a. the suspension bridge (not recommended for people over forty); (6) the good-natured group effort, with one person standing in each state, the group holding hands. The guardrails around the monument, which appear to be of recent vintage, cause me to wonder if people also used to park in four states at once.

My attention is drawn back to the monument by the antics of a carload of young French-speaking tourists. Specifically, two women in their twenties are cavorting on the monument, one of them wearing a bikini, cowboy boots, and a cowboy hat and shouting "giddyup" as she rides the other like a horse. For her part the horse snorts and whinnies and rears up on her knees, trying to throw her tormentor to the ground. A third member of the group records the event on videotape, while a handful of upright Americans watches the spectacle with uncomprehending smiles fixed on their faces.

7:15 PM. Traffic has slowed to a trickle, and most of the vendors are packing up for the day. I walk over to say good-bye to Loretta and thank her for her time.

"Tell your friends where you got your cap," she says cheerfully as she climbs in her van.

I make a final expedition to the outhouses and notice that four or five RVs are still parked in their designated lot, apparently intending to spend the night. I wave to an elderly man in plaid pants barbecuing chicken under a striped awning that extends from the side of his vehicle. He flicks his basting brush in my direction, returning my greeting. He looks happy as a clam.

To the west the sun is sinking toward the horizon, casting the landscape in amber. Far beyond the parking lot, out toward Red Mesa, an old Navajo woman wearing a pleated skirt, velveteen blouse, and bright scarf walks slowly up a hillside, holding a stick in her hand, rustling it in the bushes, herding her sheep home for the night.

Angel Fire

R ay, Susan, and I leave Santa Fe early in the morning, before the sun has cleared the mountains, driving north through Española and along the river road to Taos. Sitting in the back seat, listening to their familiar, good-natured banter, I watch the landscape roll past: ocher-colored clay hills, muted in the gray light; fields of alfalfa and hay sprouting out of winter stubble; dark, still-leafless peach and apple orchards; and rough-barked cottonwoods, their branches tipped with pale green buds. Early spring in northern New Mexico.

Just south of Taos we turn east on the town bypass and cross a lavender sage flat toward the shadowy, snow-capped Sangre de Cristo Mountains. The bypass joins U.S. 64, funnels into Taos Canyon, and begins climbing through bright meadows and dark stands of pine and fir, following a rushing trout stream. We pass ramshackle cabins and teepees with Volkswagen buses parked out front, and driveways leading across bridges to rustic chateaux, the summer homes of bankers from Amarillo and Fort Worth.

"The local dope dealers too," says Ray, who has spent a lot of time in Taos since he first came to New Mexico in 1974. "Come up here any day of the week, and the cars are home."

Though Ray seems an old friend, I've known him for only three years, since we first worked together for the Park Service at Chaco Canyon. Back in the early '70s, long before I met him, he served a two-year hitch in the army, including fourteen months in Vietnam. Bearded, burly, and wearing a Saint Louis Cardinals baseball cap with custom beadwork around the brim and a Harley-Davidson T-shirt under his denim jacket, he seems in many ways a typical, or even stereotypical, Vietnam vet. He collects underground comics and Vietnam memorabilia, and his musical taste runs to Merle Haggard and the Fabulous Thunderbirds. On occasion he seems a rough character, running with the biker crowd in Santa Fe, where he lives now, or swaggering in Evangelo's Bar, but that is mostly bravado. He is solicitous and protective of Susan, his second wife (and a woman half his size), and thoughtful and generous with his friends, often sending unannounced gifts through the mail, always willing to lend a hand around the house. It was Ray who first told me about Victor Westphall and the Vietnam veterans chapel at Angel Fire, and he who offered to drive me up here today to talk to its founder.

The highway crests at Palo Flechado Pass, then switches back and forth steeply down into the Moreno

Valley, a vast, grassy plain suspended high in the mountains. The downhill runs of the developing ski resort scratch the forested ridge enclosing the south end of the valley. "Time-share available," a billboard announces, and a second exhorts us to "ski the high country."

From a distance the chapel appears a small white sail on the sea of grass. At the turnoff a blue-and-red logo on white gates identifies it as the DAV Vietnam Veterans National Memorial. The dirt road winds around and up a knoll to the site itself, which commands an expansive view of the surrounding valley and mountains. To the northwest, over a lower ridge, I glimpse the summit of Wheeler Peak, the highest in New Mexico.

The place has changed since my last visit, since the Disabled American Veterans organization assumed financial control and management of the site. Now the three of us step through automatic sliding-glass doors into an underground visitor center, its exhibits still incomplete, and, outside again, walk toward the chapel itself along a curving cement path lined with small plaques bearing the names of men killed in Vietnam. A chilly April breeze comes up and sweeps the grass briskly; after it subsides, the site seems eerily silent.

Even close up, the chapel does not overwhelm. Designed by a Santa Fe architect named Ted Luna, it seems at best a modest imitation of Le Corbusier's Notre Dame du Haut. Its floor plan is triangular, its roof line sweeping upward from its northern base to a southern apex. At the apex a narrow window extends from floor to ceiling. Standing inside the chapel, looking out that window, one can see across the Moreno Valley, over the frenetic construction activity at the resort, to the mountains and clear, hard-blue sky beyond.

At seventy-three Victor Westphall radiates energy and good health. He is a short, robust man, with a windblown complexion and an almost leprechaunish air. Initially, he does not seem as prepossessed as I expected, or as impersonal. If a crusader, at least he is a genial one. As we sit in his new office in the visitor center, he fiddles with his pipe and we chat comfortably about the chapel and his involvement with it. He explains that the DAV began its financial support in 1977, pledging $10,000 a year for ten years. Then, in 1983, the organization offered a $2-million endowment to build the visitor center and maintain the chapel. Feeling that he had done all he could do on his own, Westphall deeded over the property and relinquished the exclusive control he had exercised over the site since he had begun construction of the chapel almost fifteen years before. Today he remains as director-for-life, with some influence over a DAV-appointed board but no individual decision-making power.

When I ask about the recent changes on site, he pauses for a minute, measuring his response, before answering. He finally allows that he doesn't care for the design of the new visitor center, which he fears will overshadow the chapel itself, but says that he recognizes the need for compromise. He has accepted most of the changes, he says, as an inevitable part of the transition from family chapel to national memorial.

"We have to learn to resolve conflicts on a per-sonal level before we can accomplish anything on an international level," he says with an air of finality, as if instructing a novice in a religious order.

For a moment, sitting quietly behind his desk, his pipe smoke suffusing the room, Westphall seems at peace with his decision and his new role. When I ask about the music that used to play softly in the chapel and over the grounds, however, his face colors suddenly and his manner intensifies.

"I told them we should keep the music, I told them it was an important part of the atmosphere, but they didn't agree. A lot of people have asked about it. If you feel strongly, you should write a letter to the board. I'm afraid I can't do anything about it."

The soundtrack that used to play softly in the chapel and over the grounds was compiled and recorded by his younger son Douglas and consisted of songs pop-ular in 1968, the year that David Westphall, Victor's older boy, was killed in a Viet Cong ambush in Con Thien, South Vietnam.

Ray is a gregarious person and likes to have peo-ple over, and he likes to play to the crowd. Drink in one hand and cigar in the other, he struts around his living room, wrapping his arm around other people's shoulders and mouthing off flamboyantly about politics, sports, whose ass he's going to kick next.

"Me llamo Ray-mundo," he announces to his audience at odd intervals in a sonorous voice, drawing out the syllables deliberately for comic effect, "and you'll never take me alive."

Friends of mine who were visiting Chaco at the time still talk about a party at which Ray, clad in bikini briefs (a gag birthday gift), an olive raincoat, and old combat boots performed an impromptu bump-and-grind to the tune of "Satisfaction," a sort of bizarre parody of an army USO show. People remember Ray and laugh when they talk about him. He is one of the extravagant characters we occasionally meet in life.

But there is a less theatrical side to him as well. Most of the people who meet Ray at a party never learn that he has a master's degree in anthropology, his thesis a study of rural auctioneers in western Kentucky and Tennessee. Most don't know that he is an avid reader of literary fiction and books about American history. And most would be surprised to find him sitting by himself late at night in unapproachable silence—his audience gone home, the performer after hours—his face transformed by inarticulate sadness, a faraway look in his eyes.

Victor Westphall is given to speaking in biblical terms, and although he would never describe himself publicly in this manner, he sees himself as a kind of apocalyptic prophet. As we sit in his office on this placid April morning, he expounds on his version of Armageddon.

"We are at a crucial juncture in history," he says deliberately, "a time when we, the human species, will choose to live or die. The crosscurrents of history are converging. We are approaching the moment of ultimate historical reckoning."

As he speaks, he stares straight at me, locking me tightly in his gaze. When he is finished, he rises from his chair, searches through a cabinet behind his desk, and hands me a slender paperback book he recently wrote and, according to an insert, published at his own expense. In its foreword Westphall states outright that he conceived it as "a manifesto." It is uncopyrighted, the better to ensure its wide distribution, and its cover features a grainy photograph of a nuclear explosion. It is called *The People's Revolution for Peace.* In it I find the following statement formatted as verse: "At the present moment in history / Civilization lacks the moral restraint / And practical intelligence to refrain / From building the nuclear tools of its own destruction." That sober, moralistic tone persists throughout. For all his sobriety, however, Westphall is not a fatalist, and he quickly rallies us to action with inspirational rhetoric: "If we bestir ourselves swiftly and courageously, / We can prevail. / The issue is for us to decide. / The question before us is not only our survival, / But our worthiness to survive."

Westphall's interest in history and historical momentum is long-standing. As a young World War II veteran and later a successful real estate developer in Albuquerque, he completed a Ph.D. in history at the University of New Mexico. The university press eventually published two of his books, scholarly studies of the public domain in New Mexico and Hispanic land grants in the upper Rio Grande region.

I recall that during my previous visits a large white cross dominated the front of the chapel, the bare cement floor under it serving as a Spartan altar. At Westphall's urging the cross has been removed. "In this age," he says tersely, "we should speak more to universality." When I ask if he considers himself a Christian, he responds, as seems his mode, by searching out and reading aloud a selection from another of his books, this one published by a vanity press and titled *What Are THEY Doing to MY World?*:

> To me God is the sum total of everything that ever was, is now, and will be, all interacting in accordance with the conscious will of all past, present, and future thought processes. I believe that somehow—I do not pretend to know how—those thought processes can and do shape the course of that which they interact upon, therefore each of them in its own way is responsible to all others.
>
> I trust that a soul force attends each physical form that is born, lives, and dies, and that it is perpetuated after death. . . .

True to his pantheism Westphall believes that spiritual forces imbue our world, and he believes that the convergence of such forces marks certain places on the earth as special. With obvious pride he explains that many of the aboriginal peoples of the area have considered the Moreno Valley sacred, and his voice becomes animated as he describes the Catholic shrine, built long ago on the chapel site by some nameless priest or Penitentes, that he dismantled by hand before beginning construction of the chapel. He gestures toward Wheeler Peak and, below it but out of sight from us, Blue Lake, held sacred by the Taos Indians and reclaimed by them from the U.S. Forest Service in 1970 following a long and celebrated legal and political battle. The chapel site, he explains, is in line with those two landmarks and partakes of the same "pipeline of spiritual energy," which Westphall envisions as a sort of conduit to the world's soul.

Sober and serious, Ray and I have never discussed religion or God, and, so far as I know, he is not a particularly religious person, at least not in the sense of holding to any systematic beliefs or going to church regularly. He and Susan (herself a down-to-earth midwesterner) were married in a simple civil ceremony, and his everyday language is emphatically profane. When we worked at Chaco, Ray and I and our other friends took great pleasure in mocking the pretentious and smug New Age spirituality that many visitors brought to the canyon. Ray had been a law enforcement ranger at an urban park in Saint Louis before transferring to Chaco, and he has little patience with people who think they have insights the rest of us lack. When he returned to Chaco to work crowd control during the Harmonic Convergence in 1987, he issued a citation to a divinity student from Harvard who had violated park regulations by climbing Fajada Butte, a prominent landmark in the park that had been closed to protect the prehistoric Anasazi sites near its summit.

"That guy was a real asshole," Ray says, his usual humor conspicuously absent. "He kept backtalking me and telling me that he had a right to do it because he understood the spiritual significance of the place. If he'd opened his mouth one more time, I'd have cuffed him and thrown his ass in jail."

Victor Westphall has always relished the attention generated by his chapel project, and he has long taken advantage of media interest in it to issue public pronouncements. In a 1972 interview with Gloria Emerson that appeared in the *New York Times*, he described the unfinished chapel as a monument to peace, not a memorial to war, and declared that if he discovered that the person who had killed his son had been killed in turn, he would place that person's photograph in the chapel alongside his son's. "I am not singling out the North Vietnamese, but I am not excluding them," he said. And he added that the chapel, which he had already named the Vietnam Veterans Peace and Brotherhood Chapel, is "for all Vietnam veterans, wherever they may be; the living, the dead, and the maimed in body and spirit."

Given Westphall's personal investment in the chapel, it isn't surprising that he feels a sense of competition with the Vietnam Veterans Memorial in Washington, D.C. When I ask whether he thinks the black granite wall embedded in the mall in Washington is an effective memorial, he remarks, somewhat peevishly, that his perception of it is influenced by what the veterans themselves think, "that it looks like a hole in the ground, and they said they've spent enough time in holes in the ground." He also believes that Jan Scruggs, the man who organized the grassroots movement that eventually produced the Washington memorial, kept some money that was intended for Angel Fire but mistakenly donated to him. Westphall maintains that the veterans themselves, "the people who know," acknowledge Angel Fire as the "true memorial."

In one sense he may be right. Although visitation to the chapel is small compared to that at the memorial in Washington, the chapel project has always struck close to the hearts of the veterans. The idea of a single man struggling alone to complete "a monument to peace" without the help or approval of the government probably has appealed to many veterans as a symbol of their own struggles to make peace with the past. Certainly no one has ever questioned Westphall's heartfelt empathy with the veterans.

Ray likes to tell the story of how he and a friend stopped at the chapel late one winter night on their way to Taos and chanced to meet Westphall, then living in a trailer on the site. Westphall invited them into his trailer, made them coffee, chatted with them. In the course of conversation he told them that several years before, when he had been in the habit of securing the chapel for the night, he had found a crudely lettered note on a piece of scrap plywood outside the chapel entrance one morning. "Why did you lock me out when I needed to come in?" the note pleaded.

"Ever since then," Westphall told them, "I just haven't had the heart to lock it up."

During its early years especially, the chapel embodied Westphall's vivid personal anguish. It was a part of a man's heart opened to the world, a quiet chamber where other men seemed comfortable in their grief. A place where men allowed themselves to remember and cry. A place, as another friend of mine says, for talking to the dead. Not a memorial to war, but a memorial to the men killed in a war.

Under the DAV's auspices the chapel is changing. Already its morbid air has been dissipated, its atmosphere depersonalized. In addition to eliminating the recorded music, the DAV has removed the portrait photographs of men killed in Vietnam—on one visit I counted 125 of those photographs—from the interior rear wall of the chapel. According to Westphall, the photographs of the men killed in his son's unit on that May day in 1968 will be placed on the wall if he is able to obtain the photographs from the Department of Defense or the men's families.

As he speaks, however, I find myself doubting whether the DAV will allow such an idiosyncratic gesture. Although the chapel will contain an altar, I also find myself wondering if the new altar will attract the kinds of messages and tokens that the area around the cross formerly did. Always one would find there a startling collection of personal artifacts: shell casings, campaign ribbons, a Frisbee, a bandanna, a snapshot of a group of friends in-country, some of the faces circled and labeled "KIA." The messages, handwritten in a notebook at the foot of the cross, were particularly, peculiarly fascinating—sometimes maudlin, sometimes sanctimonious, sometimes infinitely touching. They were the testaments of common people, written in the language of an era now long past, addressed to people now long dead. Some of them I will carry with me a long time:

> 11-11-83 / Remembering, missing, + loving my brother, Sgt. Bennie D. Begay a.k.a. Dave Lewis who did 3 1/2 tours in Nam in the Rangers, 25th Inf. Div. He was proud, and lonely. He did great there. He came home alive but paid w/his peace of mind, + his legs. He left this world in 8-81, a late victim of the damage. God Bless you Dave. Dianna said to tell you hi. I miss you bro.

Ray was born and raised across the river from Saint Louis in South Roxana, Illinois, his father a milkman, his mother a department store sales clerk. He grew up on the prairies of the Midwest, among cornfields stretching to the banks of the Mississippi, oblivious to the nearby factories of war. He enlisted in the army in 1969 after graduating from the local state college.

"It was that or get drafted and end up in the Marines," he says with a shrug. "My deferment was gone. The recruiter guaranteed me the army if I enlisted."

During 1970–71 he served fourteen months in Vietnam—more than the standard tour—in exchange for an early-out, the chance to get out of the army six months before his hitch otherwise would have been up. During his tour he worked for the most part with a company of army engineers at Long Binh and, from what I gather, saw little combat during that time. But he rarely talks in any detail about his experiences in-country, deflecting questions with glib generalizations and by repeating aloud, with a self-mocking smile and tone, his limited and highly obscene Vietnamese vocabulary. Sometimes he tells funny stories about the fringes of the war—R and R in Bangkok and Hong Kong, fistfights with lower-rank officers, military snafus. He laughs about what a crazy war it was. Still the details refuse to surface.

I feel badly that I, his friend, don't know what he saw and did there and can't do anything to help him, if in fact he wants or needs help. But I can say this: Like everyone who went there in their youth, that place changed him forever and haunts him in some manic, ill-defined way. Its oppressive, decadent atmosphere bore down on him and imprinted images on his brain. A kid from the working-class suburbs of Saint Louis sees the world in chaos, its norms twisted beyond recognition, and is changed in ways he never expected. Afterward life seems not what it was supposed to be.

We like to tease Ray that he deserved a medal for ingesting more mood- and mind-altering substances than anyone else in Vietnam, and he takes our kidding good-naturedly, but I sense that we should go only so far. Vietnam was one of the most important formative events in his life, and we, his friends, do well to remember and respect that.

Victor Westphall was operating a backhoe on his property in the Moreno Valley—property he was beginning to develop into a "mountain recreational subdivision"—on May 27, 1968, when a government sedan approached and stopped, and two Marine Corps captains emerged with the news that his older son David had been killed five days earlier in Vietnam. At the time of his death David was a twenty-eight-year-old Marine Corps first lieutenant and a veteran of a previous hitch in the Corps. He had reenlisted in late 1966 because, according to his father, he believed that "the line must be drawn somewhere against the spreading threat of world Communist domination." David was his father's son, or perhaps Victor is his son's father: By the time David died, he was already composing Biblical-sounding prose poems, excerpts from two of which his father has displayed beside the chapel's entrance.

Jeanne Westphall, David's mother, originally suggested using her son's life insurance money to build a veterans chapel. Just a month after his funeral, however, she was stricken by the first of the hysteria-producing nightmares which, according to her husband, forced her to move from the Moreno Valley to Albuquerque. Except to visit, she has never returned. Her chapel idea captured her husband's imagination, though, and he devoted himself to the project with a convert's zeal, abandoning his business, forsaking his family, and eventually moving to the trailer on the construction site to oversee work better. The chapel became his passion, his struggle, his grail.

For Victor Westphall work on the chapel has always been driven by supernatural forces. Early on, for example, he came to believe in the thaumaturgic power of the number thirteen. In *David's Story: A Casualty of Vietnam*, his painfully detailed book about his son's life and death, Westphall recalls that on March 13, 1969, during a period of utter disconsolation, when the project seemed hopelessly stalled, a burned-out light fixture miraculously began working as he arose at dusk to leave the chapel. At that moment, he says, he "knew that nothing could stop the Chapel effort." Inexplicably, he also

> realized that there must be thirteen photos of deceased Vietnam veterans in the Chapel, that the cross therein must be 13 feet high, and that we must fly a 13 star flag—the original flag of our nation. I was born on October 13, 1913, and that number had repeatedly marked significant events in my life. . . .

Westphall's conviction was reinforced when he discovered the following year that thirteen men from David's company, each from a different state, had been killed in the ambush in which his son had died.

Shortly after his son's death Westphall also received the first of his dream visitations from David. Those visitations continued for seven years, until, with the chapel well established, David "signed off." In some of those dreams David appeared as he had in life, young and vital, to encourage his father to continue work on the chapel. In others he appeared mysterious and mute, his head scarred (as it had been from the wound that had killed him), seeming a ghost of the living person. The recurrence of those visitations gradually led Westphall to conclude that he "was to be a vehicle for the transmission of ideas and action into [the chapel's] construction." Slowly, as years passed and the chapel neared completion, he came to see the project as a metaphor for the ultimate project of world peace and to see his own role in even broader terms. His ordained mission, he realized now, was to aid the end of conflict, whether it be conflict between people or nations.

These are busy days for Victor Westphall. The DAV Vietnam Veterans National Memorial will be dedicated officially soon, and much work remains to be done. At the moment Westphall is awaiting the arrival of the new exhibits for the visitor center, which are being assembled by a professional designer hired by the DAV. Westphall hopes that the exhibits, incorporating some of the tokens and messages left by visitors to the chapel, will help compensate for the rather impersonal new building.

I apologize for taking up so much of his time and rise to leave. Westphall stands and presses copies of two of his books into my hands, then sees me to the door. Outside we meet Ray and Susan, waiting patiently for me, their curious friend. Ray, suddenly shy, averts his eyes like a little boy as he tells Westphall about their previous meeting. Westphall instantly brightens and insists on giving us a tour of his apartment in the visitor center before we say good-bye.

Outside again in the cool spring air I tell Ray that I'd like to take a last look in the chapel before we head back to Santa Fe. Inside, the stuccoed walls have been stripped bare in preparation for repainting, and a vague antiseptic smell hangs in the air. The rear wall is empty. I walk to the front, where the altar will be—

where the cross used to be—and stand looking out the narrow vertical window. Across the highway I can see the runway of the airstrip at Angel Fire and, beyond it, the construction activity at a lodge at the resort. Traffic hurries by on the highway below, but no one turns to make the journey up the knoll.

As I often have in the past, I find myself thinking about Ray and the curious dislocation that Vietnam wrought in his life. From a suburb of Saint Louis to a sodden jungle in southeast Asia to a life that will always be colored by that gray-green, faraway, deadly place: an emblem of an era in our lives. In a much different way Vietnam's distant horror transformed Victor Westphall's life. Out of a real estate developer with an avocational interest in history emerged a self-ordained prophet with a mission in the world and a belief that he can change the course of history. I think about Ray's unspoken pain and Westphall's convulsive grief, about one man's silence and another's obsession, about two lives pulled far from their orbits by the gravity of a long-ago war.

I watch the traffic below.

Christic in the Desert

N orth of Santa Fe and Española, along the flanks of
the Jemez Mountains, the landscape turns harsh
and wintry. Snow blankets the ground, and dirt
roads off the highway slash the world's white
membrane, blood oozing from the earth below.
Beyond San Juan Pueblo, beyond the volcanic extrusion
of Black Mesa, beyond the deserted turnoff for El Rito,
the highway follows the Rio Chama, flowing cold and
clear over a cobbled bottom. Then, a few miles past
Bode's Store, just below Abiquiu Dam, it climbs out of
the valley onto Ghost Ranch mesa, and the view opens
up. Off to the west, across a sweep of snowy range, I can
see the frozen shoreline of Abiquiu Reservoir and,
upstream from the reservoir, the mouth of the Rio
Chama canyon. Just beyond Ghost Ranch I turn left
onto Forest Road 151, paved only here, at the intersection, and head west toward the canyon.

The road is plowed but snow-packed, smoother and faster than I have ever known it. Three miles up it bends north into the mouth of the canyon and begins tracking the river upstream. (A culvert now bridges an arroyo where, seven years ago, I turned back one wet September morning rather than chance a crossing. That morning I encountered at this spot a young woman driving alone into the canyon. Before turning around, I watched her negotiate the tricky washout and continue up the deserted road. Through the years since, I've often wondered if she made her destination.) For the next ten miles the road curves around and dips across tributary drainages, hugging the steep side of the canyon. Except for one sloppy hill where I slide close to the edge before my tires grab and my car waggles back toward the up-slope side, it is in remarkably good condition. Finally, thirteen miles from the highway, across from the confluence of the Chama and the Rio Gallina, where the canyon widens into a short valley, it enters onto private land owned by the Catholic Church, by the Benedictine Monastery of Christ in the Desert.

Here at the end of the road I park, get out, and stretch, glad to have made it. The sun is settling toward the rim of the mesa, and the oblique light, transmitted through dry, clear air—air as transparent and hard as cut glass—renders the landscape in exquisite relief and detail. The ocher and mauve strata in the sandstone cliffs appear as sharply defined, contrasting bands, and each piñon tree on the mesa, each boulder on the talus slope at the base of the cliffs, each cottonwood tree on the bottomland by the river casts a precise, individual shadow on the snow around it. Visually, the effect is of colorful objects, distinct and whole, against a black-and-white background. Emotionally, I am overcome by a strange euphoria—a desire to embrace this landscape, incorporate it, carry it away with me when I leave.

My friends wonder why I've come here. Curiosity, I tell them. The voyeuristic impulse. "To hang out with the monks and see what turns 'em on," I say mischievously. And in part that is true. But there are other, personal reasons as well.

Since I moved into Albuquerque from Chaco Canyon two and a half years ago, my work has occupied my attention and kept me in the city much of the time. I have come here to escape that closed, artificial world for a couple of days and reestablish contact with *la tierra firme*. The earth, the land.

I know of no better place to do that. Over the years, through the course of previous visits, the monastery—not the buildings themselves, of course, but the landscape in which they dwell, this lovely, lonely valley—has become, in my mind's eye, an exalted place, a remnant of Eden. And the epitome of the beauty, isolation, and mystery that distinguish the New Mexican landscape.

This particular visit has additional significance. I accepted a job in Arizona recently, and I know now that in a few months I will be leaving New Mexico. Not a big move geographically, perhaps, but one that symbolizes for me a growing up and a leaving behind. And so I have come here to say good-bye—to New Mexico and, at the same time, in a less direct and obvious way, to a person I knew and loved in Chaco, long ago, it seems, in a different life.

After unloading my bags, I walk up the road onto the grounds to locate my room—my monastic cell—and settle in for the weekend. The guest house, the first building I come to, is of typical New Mexican construction, with clay-colored stucco walls and a flat roof supported by vigas of hewn ponderosa pine. A condensation of the landscape. On one of its outside walls an effigy of Christ, delicately carved from cylinders of wood and painted in excruciating, faithful detail, hangs on a heavy wooden cross, its head crowned by thorns, its eyes closed against the pain. A sign under the bell at the gate to the courtyard instructs me to ring for the guest master. I ring once—a hard, metallic tone that doesn't resound through the canyon as I expected, but rather disappears quickly into space. I look toward the chapel, another quarter-mile up-canyon. No sound, no movement. The whole compound appears deserted, so I wander through the gate into the courtyard, open on two sides. A more primitive effigy of Saint Francis, long-robed and arms outstretched, stands in the center of the courtyard against a background of mesa and sky. Walking around the portico, I discover the communal bathroom, a gas heater warming its interior space, and two doors down, a card with my name written on it taped to the door of one of the sleeping rooms. The door is unlocked, so I enter and deposit my bags on the bed.

The cell is bare-walled and cement-floored, with one small curtained window. It is furnished, in addition to the narrow bed, with a simple wooden desk, a chair, a wardrobe, and a wood-burning stove. A stack of neatly cut firewood sits in the corner, along with a stack of newspaper and a box of matches. With no electricity, the kerosene lamp on the desk will be the only source of light after sunset. Even now, in the late afternoon, the room is dark and cold, appropriately Spartan.

Taped to the side of the wardrobe is a schedule of the day's office, which begins with vigils at 4:30 AM and concludes with compline at 7:00 PM. Work is scheduled for the morning after terce, and the main meal for the early afternoon after sext. I recall that a friend of mine, a devout Catholic who lives in Gallup, told me that the monks here are some of the few in this country who still observe the complete office every day. "They do good work up there," he said seriously. "Prayer is good work." And he explained the significance of the office to me by observing that all over the world, every day of the year, monks and priests repeat the same words, send the same message of glorification to God, a kind of worldwide hallelujah chorus.

As the hour for vespers is approaching, I begin to walk toward the chapel, still wondering about the conspicuous absence of people and a bit unnerved by the eerie silence in the canyon. Some of my trepidation is caused by the fact that I'm not Catholic, not even lapsed, and have never been to Catholic services or mass. So I don't know what to expect. I also saw the film *The Name of the Rose* recently, and I can't help picturing, only half-seriously (but half-seriously), grotesque-looking monks concealing dreadful secrets and doing strange deeds in their isolated communities.

Close to the chapel, however, I hear, through its carved oaken doors, the faint, lovely sounds of choral singing. I open one of the doors, enter a narthex, and make my way forward to an octagonal nave, in the center of which a large marble-topped table serves as an altar. The ceiling of the nave is high and its space airy, and the day's final light pours in through large clerestory windows. Through the eastern windows I can see the top of the cliff and, silhouetted against the sky, a lone cross. Of the nave's eight sides, every other one is walled. Like the western side through which I entered, the one opposite is an outward passage, and the two on the perpendicular axis extend into closed alcoves, each containing a small altar. Another carved effigy of Christ on the cross—this one painted in rather gruesome medieval fashion, blood dripping the length of its body—hangs on the southeast wall below the clerestory, cross-hatched by the shadows of the window sashes. An effigy of John the Baptist stands nearby, in a small niche in the northeast wall.

Low wooden stools line the walled sides of the nave, and a small, dark, bearded man in hooded monk's habit directs me to sit along the northwest wall with another person wearing a habit of different cloth. Each stool contains, on a shelf below the seat, a binder of psalms and another of psalms, hymns, and canticles. A monk sitting along the northeast wall accompanies the singing with a guitar, strummed lute-like. This man, gaunt, bearded, and stern-looking, resembling D. H. Lawrence during his Taos sojourn, also instructs us which page of which book to use. The singing is antiphonal, the three of us along the northwest wall joining the three monks sitting along the northeast wall, and alternating with the four along the southwest wall. Along the southeast wall, under the effigy of Christ, no one sits.

The sound is lovely, the monks' voices high, soft, and quavering, gentle and almost feminine. Between songs we pause for a moment in silence, and during those moments the chapel fills with that hushed absence of sound so characteristic of holy places, chambers of worship. "The kind of quiet you hear only in church," a friend of mine once wrote, recalling childhood Sunday mornings with his long-dead father. "A clean contained sound that must be just the element for communicating over great distances." Toward the end of the office one of the monks offers aloud a prayer for "all of our brothers who are away" and another for Father Aelred Wall, the monastery's founder, and "for all of our other brothers who have passed beyond this world"; and as we respond in song to the latter, it seems to me that at this moment the veil between the here and the hereafter is thin indeed.

The monks exit the eastern passage, but the one who instructed me where to sit, Brother Gabriel, the guest master, tells me to wait outside the western entrance until the bell is rung, signaling that I may enter the convento, the adjacent building, for the light meal.

"We eat in silence," Brother Gabriel says with some haste, his eyes darting back and forth like a sparrow's, "except for the reader. When the prior strikes his gavel on the table, the reading will stop. Take your time but finish your meal. Then leave your dishes on the table." He turns quickly and goes to catch the other monks.

I wait outside with the man who sat next to me during vespers, who introduces himself as Father Gregg Tipton, from the village of Mora. Like me, he is a visitor here, staying for a week. He is a young priest, in his thirties, and, like all of the monks, sports a healthy beard. He has removed his habit and now is wearing a down jacket on top of jeans and lug-soled hiking boots. He could be a salesman in a camping equipment store. I must confess that I feel very funny addressing him as "Father" but don't know what else to do. So "Father" it is.

"I admire the monks so much," he says gravely. "They give up so much to be here. Society, civilization, even their families. Of course," he adds, apparently to reassure me, "they may go home for two weeks each year to visit. But they give up so much. They're trying to go back to the old ways of the Benedictine order. Living simply and primitively. Eating vegetarian meals. They're living in the wilderness, for God."

He pauses a minute, then decides to leaven the mood. "The monks may seem staid and serious," he says, "but when they're just sitting around together, they're cutups. Oh yes." He chuckles but doesn't offer to elaborate.

I ask about the man who was leading the singing, the one who looks like D. H. Lawrence, a man who was—Lawrence, that is—enchanted by the flesh.

"That's Father Stephen. He's the prior. He's the only priest in residence now. He's been here a long time. Probably . . . hmm, probably about fifteen years. He's gone a lot these days. To Washington, to Rome. He'll be leaving for Mexico Sunday morning. The sister monastery at La Soledad is having a hard time, and Father Stephen is going down to welcome a new monk."

I begin to have a sense of the church hierarchy, even here, which prompts me to ask if all of the monks are equal, of the same degree of monkhood.

"Oh no. They're in various stages of commitment. The ones in the full black cowls—Timothy, Marcus, and William—have taken their final vows. One of the brothers, Christian, is in Rome now, studying for the priesthood. Gabriel's been here for about three years; I think he's taken his simple vows. Richard is a postulant; he just arrived in November. And Father Luke is visiting from Ireland.

"There's also a hermitess living here," he continues. "Ellen. The monastery received special dispensation from Rome for her to stay in one of the houses by the river. Sometimes she comes up to pray with the brothers. She may come up to mass in the morning."

My curiosity is piqued. How long has she been a hermitess?

"Oh, two or three years. Before she came here, she raised twelve children in California. Then she felt the calling and made the decision to leave her family. Her husband comes to visit a couple of times a year. I've met him several times during my visits."

He senses my interest. "Of course, they no longer may have intimate relations but must live as brother and sister."

As I ponder the life of a hermitess, Father Gregg asks me if I've visited the monastery previously.

Yes, I tell him, several times, but never overnight, and I've never attended prayers with the brothers.

"Are you Catholic?" he asks suddenly.

I admit that I'm not. In fact, I admit that I find the whole subject of religion very confusing.

"Ah, you're searching," he interprets.

I say nothing, weighing my answer, reluctant to mislead him or evade his question but also reluctant to be completely honest about my idiosyncratic beliefs.

He senses my discomfiture. "Just Christian then," he says with a nervous laugh.

With that the bell rings, and we make our way to the convento. En route to the dining room we pass through the monastery's library, comparable in size to a small high school's and smelling faintly of lamp oil and old books, a heady elixir. My curiosity is aroused, and I decide to set aside some time tomorrow to investigate.

For the meal we sit on wooden benches around the outside of a U-shaped wooden table. Two of the monks serve us homemade bread, butter, broccoli soup, and hot tea, and as we eat by flickering candlelight, a gray-haired, gray-bearded, scholarly looking monk with wire-rimmed glasses sits at a side table reading aloud from a book called *Treasures in Earthen Vessels: The Vows*. It is a serious book about spiritual commitment and the temptations of the flesh, and I am surprised by its frank discussion of the evils of, among other things, masturbation. The monks seem to listen attentively and absorb the message, and I once again find myself imagining all kinds of sordid goings-on in the monastic cells, everything from pornography to self-flagellation. I also recall once meeting a woman who, when she was younger, had been a nun for seven years. "For those seven years," she said, summing up her experience, "I thought about nothing but men." I laughed at the time, thinking she only confirmed what I already suspected. But, it occurs to me now, perhaps the consuming desires I impute to the monks are just a projection of my own personality and life, just the predictable thoughts of an admittedly impure inhabitant of the world, corrupted by lurid movies, twentieth-century agnosticism, and the complicated pleasures of sex. And perhaps there is a purer, simpler way. Perhaps. In fact, I'd like to believe so. I really would. If not for me, at least for others.

After dinner, as I walk back alone to the guest house, an owl hoots eerily in the talus, and snow crunches underfoot. A cold night along the Rio Chama. Juniper smoke from the monks' chimneys drifts down-canyon—a powerful distillation that will always evoke for me, no matter where I am, winter nights in northern New Mexico. I make my way to my cell, stoke a fire in the stove, and climb into my sleeping bag. I close my eyes as if to pray, but sleep overtakes me quickly.

I awake at dawn, dress hurriedly in the cold room —the fire in the stove long dead—and make my way to the chapel for lauds and mass. Ellen is there, a tall, attractive woman in her late fifties, dressed in a drab, full-length habit and wearing a head wrap that completely hides her hair. Brother Gabriel surprises me by offering, after the prayer for Father Aelred, a simple prayer on my behalf. I'm touched. Then, although I have some qualms about doing so, I go through mass and take the Eucharist with them. They seem not to notice my hesitancy or not to care, and after the ritual each person embraces every other briefly and wishes them heartfelt "peace."

Breakfast is self-serve. Afterward I take a few minutes to browse through the library, which consists of a mixture of hardcover and paperback volumes, some donated, some purchased. Housed on homemade wooden shelves, the collection is eclectic and of uniformly high quality: Aristotle, Aquinas, Merton, *Primitive Christianity*, and various commentaries on the Bible; Dostoevsky, Camus, and Walker Percy; Marx, Freud, *African Genesis*, and *The Dragons of Eden*; *Blue Highways*, *Milagro* and *Tijerina and the Courthouse Raid*; field guides and foreign language dictionaries; on a reading table, recent issues of *National Geographic*, *Newsweek*, and *The Christian Science Monitor*; on a rack labeled "Recent Acquisitions," a book titled *The AIDS Cover-Up*.

Because I've offered to help with the daily work,
as guests are encouraged to do, one of the monks—Marcus, a handsome young man with blue eyes and sandy
hair and beard, who has shed his cowl and now is wearing blue jeans, a down jacket, and high gum boots—
finds me in the library and asks if I'd be willing to help
him, William, and Timothy unload a fifty-five-gallon
drum of kerosene off a truck. We walk outside and farther into the monastic compound, where visitors normally aren't permitted. The monks have backed one of
the monastery's four-wheel-drive pickups through knee-
deep snow close to a small wooden platform, on which
the tapped drum will rest so that the residents can refill
their lamps. William could be a darker version of Marcus,
with a vestigial Southern accent. Deep South, from the
sound of it. I can't help thinking that he and Marcus,
both in their thirties and both endowed with boyish
good looks, belong somewhere else, on a university cam-
pus or in a Colorado ski town. Somewhere with other
young people and at least the potential for normal social
interaction. Somewhere out in the world.

Timothy, on the other hand, seems the picture
of a real monk. I can't guess his age: fifty, fifty-five, sixty,
sixty-five. He looks like Merlin, or what I've always
imagined Merlin to look like. Long, wiry white hair
pulled behind an old T-shirt wrapped around his head
and a long, wiry white beard floating on his chest. Ruddy
cheeks that give his face an angelic aspect and blue eyes
that dance with energy and intelligence. An air of contentment, but without the infuriating smugness exhib-

ited by most people who think they know the answer. Here, it seems to me, is the genuine article. A man of God, truly. But as well he has that unmistakable look of someone who has been around the block, who is (or was) well acquainted with the devious, factitious, seductive ways of the world. And who willingly gave it all up.

For a few minutes we wrestle vainly with the drum of kerosene, which I figure weighs close to five hundred pounds, but the four of us working together finally slide, scrape, and bump it onto the platform. Then, as I turn to walk back to the guest house, Marcus asks if I'd be willing to help Richard—the scholarly looking man who was the reader at the light meal yesterday afternoon and who has just appeared at the platform—with the week's communal laundry. I agree, and for the next three hours I help Richard sort and load the laundry into the monastery's 1948 Hotpoint washing machine, rinse and wring it, and hang it on the clothesline.

Richard is close to retirement age for most professions but came to the monastery as a postulant just two months ago to begin his monastic life. He is scheduled to stay for six months, then leave for a short time while he and the community decide independently of each other whether he should take his simple vows and return on a more permanent basis. Before coming here, he worked in upper management for the Palmer House Hotel, for Illinois Bell, and, most recently, for a large insurance company, all in Chicago. But he has long been drawn to the simplicity and rigors of monastic life. He doesn't mention a wife or children, and I infer that he is a lifelong bachelor.

▼ Christ in the Desert ▼

Five years ago, after his father died—releasing him, as he puts it, from his "final parental obligation"—he began to heed his calling seriously, visiting monasteries in Vermont, Indiana, Minnesota, and Colorado before deciding to come to Christ in the Desert. Although he is for the most part a relaxed and friendly sort, he speaks about his decision to come here intently and with some zeal, like a trial lawyer summing up his case.

"Christ in the Desert is absolutely unique among American monasteries because of its adherence to the basic principles of Benedict, its primitiveness, and its isolation. I checked into the other monasteries fairly thoroughly, but all of the signs pointed here. This is where I was headed."

I ask about the principles of Benedict.

"The basic tenets are three: prayer, reading or study, and physical labor. And of course," he adds with evident pride, "all of the monks take vows of poverty." (A few minutes later, as I hang a load of clothes on the line, I discover with some amusement that although most of the monks' personal clothing is plain and well-worn, one of them wears Calvin Klein jeans.)

Richard chuckles. "We try to live simply out here, but the irony is that living simply requires a lot of time and work. Just this month both of our electric generators went out in the same day, and then when Marcus was towing one of them back from town, the trailer tipped over about five miles up the road. It took us all day to get the trailer upright and in here."

What about the division of labor?

"Oh, we share the day-to-day chores. Each person cooks one day of the week. We eat mostly vegetarian meals, but the Rule of Benedict only prohibits the consumption of 'four-footed animals,' so we may eat fish and fowl. We have two turkeys in the freezer right now. Marcus is cooking today, so we'll probably have Mexican food.

"But everybody has a special vocation too. Marcus woodworks, Gabriel is in charge of maintaining the vehicles, and Timothy is a good all-around handyman. I guess I'm in charge of the laundry," he notes wryly.

What about funding?

"The church helps support us. And we get donations. And our craft sales help, especially Marcus's woodworking. He has a backlog of commissions from well-to-do people in Santa Fe."

I tell him the monastery's library is a real asset.

"Yes, it is," he agrees, staring out the window of the laundry room, thinking. Then, without my prompting, he adds, "But this is not an intellectual place. No, not really an intellectual place. Though some here value the mind. Both Stephen and Timothy are very well-read. Timothy is a delight. An old-time monk. He simply glows with the Lord. And he's at peace with himself. You can see that. He's also very funny. We've become good friends in the time I've been here."

As he seems willing to talk about the other monks, I ask about their backgrounds.

"Marcus graduated from seminary. And William too, I think. Both of them became monks shortly after they got out of school, and both have spent sixteen or seventeen years now in monasteries. They're not worldly men," he says matter-of-factly.

"William's leaving, did you know that?" he continues, musing aloud. "Tomorrow morning. Seventeen years in monasteries, including seven here, and he's leaving. He says he wants a more activist ministry, so he's going to help a friend of his in Winnipeg who's starting a community worship center. I don't understand William. I don't think he knows what he wants," Richard says without explaining what he means, although it seems perfectly reasonable to me that a man still young might want to experience more of the world after seventeen years of cloistered devotion.

What about political or community involvement on the part of the monks, either locally or, through the church, farther afield?

"Not much really. Monasteries, of course, are not primarily political institutions. But we keep up with current events through magazines and newspapers. We don't get television or radio out here. Because of the monastery's isolation, it would be difficult to have regular interaction with any other community. This place is isolated," he says again with some relish.

Gabriel appears in the door to ask if he may borrow the truck Richard has been using in order to jump-start another one.

"I hope I do it right," he says to me with a shrug. "They just put me in charge of vehicles two weeks ago."

Gabriel seems bewildered by his new duties. He does not strike me as someone with innate mechanical ability.

Richard asks him the name of the postulant who left the monastery last year.

Gabriel thinks for a minute. "I think his name was Jim. Yeah. Jim Baca."

Richard turns to me, smiling. "He completed his postulancy, then left to tell his girlfriend that he was going to take his vows and remain at the monastery. Well, before he could tell her, she told him that she was leaving him—beat him to the punch—and we haven't seen him since."

Gabriel cackles. "Yeah, if they see their girlfriends, they're gone. The world gets 'em."

As Gabriel leaves, Timothy drops off an old, filthy jump suit with straw and twigs hanging on it.

Richard laughs. "Timothy gets more mileage out of clothes than anybody I know. He gives new meaning to the words 'monastic poverty.'"

I ask about the number of monks who have resided at the monastery over the years.

"They were up to eleven at one time, but we're down to six now, counting myself and Christian, who's in Rome studying for the priesthood. And Stephen is here less and less of the time. He's very busy these days."

Although Richard doesn't say so, I get the impression that Stephen would like to leave. Over the long term, living out here would be a wearing endeavor, regardless of the vigor of your spiritual commitment. Visiting is another matter altogether.

"This is a beautiful, wondrous place," he says. "It really is. People drag in here looking absolutely beat—the world's got their number. They come here,

some Catholic, some not, some not even Christian"—
and here I feel him look at me out of the corner of his
eyes—"to stay a week or ten days. And they leave revived
and invigorated, ready to face it all over again. You can
see it in their faces. This is a magical place."

After sext and main meal—enchiladas, beans,
rice, and flour tortillas—during which Marcus reads
aloud from a more programmatic, less provocative book
called *The Practice of Spiritual Direction*, I spend an hour
in the gift shop at the guest house, inspecting the wares.
An aphorism, painstakingly inscribed in a piece of sandstone leaning against the outside wall, sets the context
and mood: "Crafts speak of an age when dignity lay in
silence and beauty in subtlety."

Inside are displays and arrangements of crucifixes
and small icons, incense and censers, homemade greeting
cards, Pueblo Indian pottery, and shawls and scarves
woven by a monk named Jeremy, evidently now gone. A
binder holds photos of Marcus's furniture, the work of a
craftsman's hands. The selection of books includes, in
addition to a Paulist Press series called *The Classics of
Western Spirituality*, an anthology titled *Poets of
Nicaragua* and several volumes of poetry by Daniel
Berrigan. And many books by Thomas Merton, the
famous modern interpreter of monastic life. On a table
near the door I find a typed sheet containing an excerpt
from an article Merton wrote in 1968 about the recently
established Monastery of Christ in the Desert. In that
article he said:

The monastic life in Christianity is a life of hope and hardship, of risk and penance in the sense of *metanoia*, a complete inner revolution, renunciation of ease and privilege in order to work with one's hands, in the insecurity of a place remote from one's original home and even from civilization itself. . . .

[The monastery] remains a sanctuary where both monks and retreatants, Christians, believers in other faiths and those with no religious belief at all may experience something of that 'peace which the world cannot give.' But even if no one else knew of the existence of such a place, the monastery would still fulfill the purpose of its existence by singing the praise of God in the wilderness. . . .

[The Monastery of Christ in the Desert] seeks only to keep alive the simplicity of Benedictine monasticism: a communal life of prayer, study, work and praise in the silence of the desert where the word of God has always been best heard and most faithfully understood.

On another table an open wicker basket contains several hundred dollars in cash and personal checks. A sign above the table requests that guests calculate the total amount of their purchases, add state sales tax according to a posted tax table, and make their own change.

Before leaving, I peruse the guest register. During the last two years about seven hundred people have visited the monastery. Although California and Colorado are well represented, more of the visitors have been local, coming from the small Hispanic towns that dot the mountainous countryside of northern New Mexico: Ojo

Sarco, Ojo Caliente, Gallina, Coyote, Cañones, Canjilon, Tierra Amarilla. I don't recognize any names, but as I am about to leave, my eyes fasten on the signature of a woman who came to the monastery from Santa Fe last Easter Sunday. I smile at her name and hope that the person is as lovely as it is. I smile at the name of Angelica Luz.

After vespers and light meal, after compline, after darkness has overtaken the canyon and the monks have retired to their individual cells, I go for a long walk out the deserted entrance road. Although the surface was sloppy during the warm afternoon, it is frozen solid now, providing good traction and easy progress. The nighttime air is as clear and cold as ice, and innumerable stars glitter sharply overhead, each a prickling in my eye. Orion dominates the southern sky, and a moon one night past full rises over the mesa, its light reflecting off the snow and illuminating the landscape in ghostly brilliance. Across the white surface of a snowy flat, the dark shapes and shadows of juniper and piñon trees seem to conceal wonderful, terrifying mysteries. The world is soundless but for the steady crunching of my footsteps and, where the road passes close enough to its banks, the rush of the river. At one point I hear, far off, a spall of sandstone clatter in the talus, probably pried loose by moisture freezing in a hairline crack in the cliff.

A silent world of rock, snow, and stars. An ethereal, inhuman realm. One that impresses on me, as might be expected, the immensity and exquisite beauty of creation and, at the same time, its frightening impersonality.

Forces me to confront the "benign indifference of the universe," as Camus put it. My thoughts, however, are not all so rarefied. As I walk farther and farther along the road, I find myself drawn back, as if by some strange gravity, to our tiny planet, the only home we will ever know—the place where we were born, where we carry on the private struggles that are the measure of our human lives, and where we will die; and earthbound again, I find myself melancholy and cathartically self-indulgent, taking advantage of this peaceful moment to remember long-ago nights in Chaco Canyon, a person I loved there who is gone forever, and a time when the world was a heartbeat younger and life simpler and all things seemed possible.

Late at night I make my way back into the cold, silent compound, back into my cell—dark but for the moonlight filtering through the window curtain—and slip into my sleeping bag without so much as striking a match.

Upon awaking I begin to pack. After seeing the road yesterday afternoon, I've decided to get an early start before the slop thaws. Although the morning is gray and cold, breaks in the clouds promise another warm afternoon. I load the car, then walk slowly back to the chapel to spend a final few minutes in its sanctuary. Sitting on my now-customary stool, I study the image of Christ on the southeast wall, his face tortured and redemptive. The interior space over which he presides is empty and eerily quiet. As when I arrived, the monks are once again invisible. I leave the payment for my room and meals in the wicker basket in the gift shop.

▼ Christ in the Desert ▼

My car cranks and warms slowly, and I begin the long drive back to Albuquerque. The road is frozen and deserted, making for easy passage and leaving me free to enjoy the landscape and reflect on my visit. I think mostly about Marcus and William, two men my own age who have spent all of their adult years in isolated monastic communities, their lives devoted to God and devoid of the pleasures and complications of normal human society. During their long days of labor and solitude, what thoughts occupy their minds and what feelings their hearts? Can I, so different from them, even imagine such things? I think about William, leaving this morning for a new life in Winnipeg. How will he respond to the perils and temptations of the world? How will his experiences change him? Once he is gone, will he ever return to this Edenic place? This place of innocence and possibility?

As the road emerges from the canyon and crosses the new culvert over the arroyo, I remember again the cool, damp September morning seven years ago when, coming the other direction, I stopped my car and got out to investigate the stream flowing across the road in the bottom of this same arroyo. At the time I was on month-long furlough from my job in Chaco, feeling young and unencumbered, on my way to visit friends in Colorado. As I stood on the embankment, in the process of deciding not to continue, a brown Honda Civic station wagon pulled up and stopped behind my car, and I turned and walked back to talk to the driver.

She rolled down her window as I approached. She was a pretty woman in her early thirties, with creamy skin, green eyes, and shoulder-length hair the color of oak wood. And wearing a dark green wind parka, a beige turtleneck sweater, and blue jeans. Her car was packed full, with boxes and clothes piled in back.

We began to talk, first about the road and the prospects for making it to the monastery, and then about other things: the monastery itself; Chaco, where she had never visited but wanted to; the fact that she was leaving that morning for Montana after having spent the summer in Santa Fe. Moving back, she said. And something about a man—either leaving or returning to him. She spoke vaguely, and I wasn't sure which.

"I try to come out here every Sunday," she said. "Sometimes I take mass with the brothers, sometimes I just wander off by myself. I think this is my favorite place in the world. I come out here when I need to think things through."

She looked down and smiled self-consciously. "I need to get to the monastery this morning."

Soon after we began to talk, she turned off her car's engine. In the mouth of the canyon, with the sandstone walls looming over us, the morning was suddenly very quiet and still, sepulchral. As I stood in my sweatshirt beside her car, I kept my hands in my pockets to warm them, and as we spoke, our breath left wisps of vapor hovering momentarily in the damp air. The smell of sage enveloped us.

There was something intimate about our surroundings and our conversation, and something vulnerable about her. Her cheeks were downy—a child's—her voice quiet and brittle. But she wasn't afraid of me, wasn't apprehensive, as she had a right to be, meeting a strange man on a deserted road. On the contrary, she seemed to sense, as I did, that there was something mutual between us, a preexisting connection. And that somehow our meeting wasn't merely accidental. How else explain our presence on the road that morning, the myriad invisible forces that had brought each of us there, the complementary nature of our genders? She looked me in the eyes as we spoke, and I thought about leaning down and kissing her, brushing the down on her cheek with my lips.

We talked for twenty or thirty minutes before our conversation lulled. I asked her then if she was going to continue up the road. Yes, she said, staring distractedly through the windshield, she needed to get to the monastery.

Then she turned her head toward me partway and looked up shyly. "I have a tow rope," she said, smiling. "Let's go together. If we get stuck, we can pull each other out."

I looked up the canyon, considering what she said, and for a moment the world was full of possibility, and I almost answered yes, yes, of course, let's go together . . . But I was due in Boulder that evening, and I had bad feelings about the road ahead. The first three miles had been sloppy, and the mud would only get worse as it wound upriver. So I told her I wasn't going, that the venture seemed too risky, but that I would wait to make sure she got across the arroyo before I turned around. And I smiled at her then, sharing the promise of the moment.

I walked back to my car and moved it off to the side, and she passed by on my right. As I stood on the embankment, she drove slowly into the arroyo, maneuvered her car into the stream, and forded it. She revved the engine to climb out. As she accelerated up the opposite embankment, on her way, she leaned out of the window and looked back and waved. She smiled and shouted something to me. She smiled and waved.

"Piece of cake," she said.

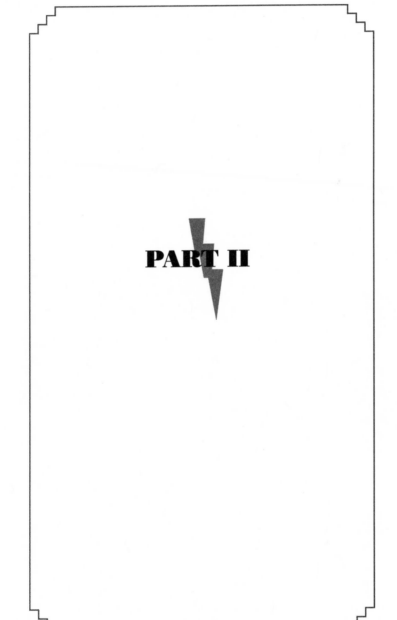

PART II

Navajo Country

From Santa Fe, where I live now, the drive to Kayenta, Arizona, south of Monument Valley in the heart of the Navajo reservation, is long and treacherous. Leaving late on a summer afternoon, one drives south on I-25 and then northwest on New Mexico 44, through the disintegrating adobe town of Cuba, across the continental divide, past the lonely turnoffs to Chaco Canyon, and into Bloomfield and Farmington at dusk. After dinner one proceeds west along the San Juan River, through the cut in the Hogback, under the vapor streetlights of the town of Shiprock, and into the darkening, twilight void of the reservation. The road becomes a two-laned roller coaster, with a potholed surface and uneven camber, and dull-eyed cattle and horses graze its steeply sloping shoulders. Past Beclabito and Teec Nos Pos the world grows ever darker, ever more foreign. "Fat sheep 4 sale," a hand-painted sign outside the deserted trading post at

Mexican Water announces, and eerie shadows of hoodoo rock loom beside the highway. Finally, seven hours and 330 miles from Santa Fe, one sees the welcome glitter of Kayenta, the familiar logos of the gas stations, the reassuring lights of the Holiday Inn.

I first drove the road from Shiprock to Kayenta in 1976, when I was traveling with friends from Mesa Verde to the Grand Canyon. On that trip I underestimated the vast distances between towns on the reservation, and we were forced to detour a short distance from the highway to the trading post at Dinnehotso, Arizona, to buy gas. My memory is of two or three Navajo men sitting on a bench in the shade of the front porch, watching us silently and with apparent disdain. I remember I was relieved that the trading post was otherwise deserted.

Then, in 1978, I went to work for the National Park Service in the Needles District of Canyonlands National Park in southeastern Utah. I often shopped in the little Mormon town of Monticello, the northernmost range of the Navajo, Ute, and Paiute Indians who inhabit that corner of the state. I encountered them at the Blue Mountain grocery store, speaking their (to me) unfamiliar languages, avoiding eye contact with strangers. I observed them closely but kept a respectful distance. My view of Indians was very romantic. I remember the disappointment I felt when I learned that the name Sweet Alice Spring—one of my favorite place names in the canyon country—was a cartographer's gloss on what the local cowboys had originally called the place: Sweet Ass Spring, because in the old days that was where they went to have a roll with the squaws from south of Elk Ridge.

If Canyonlands provided me passing contact with the Navajos, when I went to work for the Park Service at Chaco Canyon in 1980, I landed in their laps. Although Chaco is not located within the boundaries of the Navajo reservation, it is located in the heart of ancestral Navajo country. In their mythology the *Diné*—the "People"—emerged from the earth near Dzilth-na-o-dith-hle, a prominent mesa just north of the canyon, and the population of the area still is overwhelmingly Navajo.

During my five years at Chaco relations between the Navajos and the Anglos (so-called, regardless of our ethnicity) were never what one would call good. For the most part the Navajos regarded us from a distance with ill-concealed suspicion. Their attitude was due in large part to our (in their view) morbid interest in the prehistoric Anasazi ruins in the canyon, which they knew contained human burials and, therefore, the evil spirits, or *ch'inde*, that haunt places of death. Only witches muck around in ruins. Traditional Navajos still believe strongly in the existence of witches—people who have succumbed to the dark forces of the world and who seek to use, for their own evil purposes, the power of the dead.

The maintenance crew at Chaco was entirely Navajo, and for some of us who worked there and thought about such things, one of that crew seemed to embody the Navajos' otherworldly menace. Franklin was short-legged, long-waisted, and overweight, his belly hanging over his belt. His bulk seemed threatening, however, not flaccid, and his appearance was made almost fearsome by his severe crewcut and ever-present aviator sunglasses.

"Franklin's a witch," a roommate of mine who had lived on the reservation for many years and who was acquainted with such things maintained emphatically. "You can tell by the way he *watches* you. Always looking for an opportunity."

It was true. Under Franklin's baleful stare people did the stupidest things. Another roommate of mine, normally a careful, conscientious person, drove away from the gas pump in the maintenance yard with the hose still in the tank, as Franklin stared silently from the garage bay door. And if you found yourself stuck on the dirt entrance road after a rain- or snowstorm, Franklin invariably drove up, sometimes condescending to pull you out, sometimes claiming his truck lacked the necessary power and traction. Even some of the local Navajos believed Franklin was a witch, and they steered clear of him. A woman with whom I worked, one of Franklin's neighbors, blamed him for the mysterious fits of crying that awoke her in the middle of the night, and others sought the services of a medicine man to combat his evil spells.

Franklin maintained the park's water treatment system, and Randy, our park archeologist, liked to speculate that he could poison all of us and no one would discover the bodies for weeks.

"They'd probably find him reclining in the superintendent's chair, wearing a bunch of smelly skins and smoking a big cigar," Randy said.

We liked to joke about Franklin and his supposed witchery, but we also kept our distance. In Chaco Canyon one needed to be careful.

After leaving Chaco, I worked for a summer at Navajo National Monument, located thirty miles west of Kayenta, high on the airy expanse of the Shonto Plateau. In terms of social interaction the two parks were dramatically different. Whereas at Chaco the Navajos and Anglos seemed to inhabit different worlds, at Navajo the two groups mingled freely. We lived next door to each other, shared potluck dinners with each other, played volleyball with each other.

A portion of our duties at Navajo consisted of spending week-long stints, twice during the summer season, in a hogan near a backcountry site known as Keet Seel, a beautiful Anasazi cliff dwelling set in a buff-colored sandstone alcove, far up a remote, well-watered tributary of Tsegi Canyon. Keet Seel means "Broken Pottery" in Navajo, and although Richard Wetherill excavated a portion of the ruin in the spring of 1895, it still is littered with thousands of the prehistoric potsherds that inspired its name.

Although our hogan had been constructed by the Park Service from a mail-order kit, it was, by modern

American standards, primitive: no running water, no electricity, no telephone. Except for the tiresome chore of hauling water every day from a spring in an arroyo a quarter of a mile away, however, those weeks at Keet Seel were idyllic. Our primary responsibility was to show the ruin to the small groups of tourists who walked or rode horses out the eight-mile-long trail each day. Otherwise it was simple maintenance, with the mornings reserved for a cup of tea on the porch in the early sun and the evenings for reading and writing by the light of an oil lamp, listening to the crickets, toads, and coyotes—the night sounds of the canyon.

During my second stint at Keet Seel, however, my peaceful routine was interrupted by the arrival on horseback of a four-man Navajo maintenance crew, come to perform the annual stabilization work on the ruin. The crew was headed by Clarence Austin, a large, shy man who was often unexpectedly playful; like a child he delighted in sneaking up on and spooking his unsuspecting coworkers. Clarence was accompanied by Russell Dodge and William Nez, two handsome young men with shoulder-length black hair and, perhaps because both had attended college for a time, a worldly air about them. The fourth member of the crew, Andrew Laughter, was a quiet, worn-looking middle-aged man, a recovering alcoholic plagued by intractable health problems.

All of the men were friendly and likable, but Russell was special. He came from a prominent local family, his grandfather a renowned medicine man, his brother an artist of some celebrity. Russell's particular gifts were his keen intelligence and teasing sense of humor. "I was born under the sign of coyote," he liked to say, and he was indeed a trickster figure. At night, with visitors in the canyon, he mimicked the calls of coyotes and owls, and—unusual for a Navajo—he enjoyed mugging for a camera. I still have a photograph of him brushing his teeth one damp morning outside the hogan, his teeth bared and brush poised in cartoonish exaggeration. But there was a serious side to him as well. Sometimes, for no apparent reason, he withdrew from the group, not mad at anybody, just pensive and distant. Not knowing him well, I never asked what triggered those spells—at the time it seemed better to leave him alone with his thoughts.

Clarence and the crew set up camp next to the hogan and, being good, traditional Navajos, proceeded to spend the next few days diligently avoiding the ruin they had been sent to stabilize. Their day began with breakfast, always an elaborate production. Russell or William brewed potent coffee in a soot-blackened pot, while Andrew mixed and kneaded dough and cooked fry bread over the campfire, and Clarence cooked bacon or sausage on the gas stove in the hogan. After breakfast they spent an hour gathering and organizing their equipment. Most days they started work by wandering up- or down-canyon on reconnaissance missions of vague purpose, returning to the hogan a couple of hours later for lunch. After lunch they reluctantly climbed into the ruin to do some stabilization work, returning again to the hogan to wait out the late-afternoon thunderstorms by playing cards and listening to tapes on my Walkman. We ate communal dinners most nights, and then, after dinner, they began preparations for their nightly sweat.

Several years earlier some of the Navajos who worked at the park had built a small sweat lodge next to the hogan. Because the men spent a portion of each day in the ruin, they took sweats every night to cleanse themselves of the *ch'inde*. Russell began the process by stoking a campfire into which he placed small chunks of sandstone. He and Andrew then disappeared into the nearby thickets, returning a few minutes later with bunches of sage, cliffrose, piñon, and juniper which they started boiling in a bucket of water on the fire. An hour later, when all was ready, Russell gave a mock war cry, Clarence and Andrew joined in, and they quickly stripped to their underpants and crawled into the sweat lodge, sitting side by side on a rough plank bench.

After the first night they asked if I wanted to join them, and I accepted gladly. (The must and decay of the ruin also struck me as unhealthy; a purification ritual seemed a good idea.) Because William didn't participate in the sweats—I was never sure why—he was given the job of shoveling the heated rocks into a compartment in the front of the sweat lodge and pouring the bucket of herbal tea over them, filling the tiny interior space with a dense steam redolent of sage. Inside, as we sat sweaty thigh to sweaty thigh, Russell led Clarence and Andrew in traditional Navajo chants, at odd moments breaking into hand-clapping versions of "[My

Baby Does the] Hanky Panky" or something equally irreverent. We told corny jokes. They teased me that by taking sweats, I would turn brown like them. I responded, with no particular logic, that, as Todd Rundgren once said, "some folks is even whiter than me." And we laughed together. After emerging from the sweat lodge, we doused ourselves with buckets of cold water and shivered in the night air as we toweled off. Those evenings were familiar and friendly. I have never seen Navajos so relaxed, so happy, and I have never felt so relaxed around them.

One twilight evening as we were talking beside the hogan, I asked Clarence about edible plants in the area. He knelt down and with his pocketknife dug up a small tuber, which he said was a wild potato. Can you eat it? I asked. He looked up at me, his broad face—normally filled with twinkling amusement—serious and kindly.

"Oh yeah," he said softly, pausing for an instant to look me in the eye. "This is what the Navajos lived on when Kit Carson was chasin' their asses."

Another afternoon we were surprised by the arrival at the hogan of two Japanese women, come to camp overnight. They were sisters, traveling across America. Sumiko, the younger one, had arrived in the United States only recently and was shy about speaking her schoolgirl English, but her sister, Akiko, had lived in Los Angeles for several years, spoke fluent English, and served as interpreter. They were tiny women and, to save weight, had not carried a tent with them in their backpacks. Hearing that, I invited them to come to the hogan for shelter if thunderstorms developed later in the day, as often happened at that time of year.

That evening, as lightning flashed and rain poured down, Clarence, the crew, the Japanese women, and I played cards, told jokes, and talked. Perhaps because of their own remote Asian origins, the Navajo men felt an immediate though ill-defined kinship with the Japanese women. Between them there was a mutual fascination. They compared customs and languages and discussed various encounters with people of European descent, concluding that most whites were horribly prejudiced against people of color. They asked me what I thought, and I agreed. I added, however, that on occasion I found the Navajos' attitude toward outsiders equally repugnant. And without saying anything more, we seemed to reach an understanding.

The conversation turned to less onerous subjects. Akiko taught us some pidgin Japanese, and Russell a Navajo limerick. We shared one of my cigars (in lieu of a peace pipe, we joked) and stayed up late listening to the rain and enjoying the peaceful night in the isolated canyon, so distant from the expectations and limitations of mainstream society. The next morning, as Akiko and Sumiko prepared to leave, we engaged in a frantic photo session, exchanging cameras and snapping pictures of unlikely combinations of people in unlikely poses. Finally we said good-bye, and the women were gone.

Soon my week at Keet Seel ended as well. I gave Clarence my Walkman, said good-bye to the crew—feeling sadder than I had expected I would—and walked out of the canyon for the last time.

I have visited the park several times since then and seen Clarence. He still seems the same gentle, beneficent man I knew that summer. Andrew went into the Indian Health Service hospital in Tuba City for a gall bladder operation a month after our time at Keet Seel; I've been told his liver is failing now, and he's dying. I've seen William Nez a couple of times, and he is as handsome and aloof as ever. I never saw Russell again. He committed suicide the following December, shooting himself with a rifle one night by his family's corral. His relatives wouldn't go near the body, so some of the park staff buried him in a stand of piñon and juniper trees, not far from the rim of Tsegi Canyon.

By the time I worked at Navajo, I had already embarked on a new career, having completed my first year of law school in Albuquerque. Two years later, after graduation, I moved to Arizona to work for a law firm that represents the Navajo Tribe (or Navajo Nation, as it now prefers to be known) in a land dispute against the Hopis and the Southern Paiutes.

The law of that case is strange indeed. In 1934, in an effort to contain the Navajo reservation in Arizona (through various executive orders it had grown enormously since its establishment by the 1868 Navajo treaty) and consolidate the checkerboarded lands in and around it, Congress enacted a statute defining the reservation's exterior boundaries and setting aside those lands "for the benefit of the Navajo and such other Indians as may already be located thereon." The area defined by the 1934 boundary act included—but the act expressly did not affect the status of—the reservation that had been established in 1882 "for the use and occupancy of the Moqui [Hopi]. . . ."

The proximity of the two peoples is unfortunate. In addition to speaking different (and mutually unintelligible) languages, they are culturally distinct, some might say incompatible. The Hopis are a Puebloan people who continue to inhabit ancient mesa-top villages and to subsist by cultivating corn, beans, and squash; the Navajos a pastoral people organized around matrilineal family groups that often migrate seasonally, even today, between summer and winter camps. In early historic times the two groups coexisted uneasily, with occasional eruptions of violence in the form of Navajo raids on Hopi settlements and Hopi reprisals. Although physical violence became less common after the United States acquired the territory that is now northern Arizona in 1848, in this century the increasing population of both tribes has exacerbated the competition for scarce resources in their common homeland.

In 1974, because of continuing conflict between the two tribal governments, Congress authorized the United States district court in Arizona to partition the lands within the 1882 reservation known as the Navajo-Hopi Joint Use Area, thus precipitating the so-called Big Mountain dispute. At the same time, Congress authorized either tribe to file suit against the other to quiet title to the remaining lands within the 1934 reservation. Eight days later the Hopi tribe filed its complaint, claiming an undivided one-half interest in nearly all of those lands, some seven million acres in northern Arizona that until then had appeared on maps as the Navajo reservation. As a result of a decision by a federal court of appeals, the outcome of the case, which is ongoing, will turn on the reconstruction of a particular historical scene: which tribe was "occupying, possessing or using" which lands on June 14, 1934, the day when Congress passed the 1934 boundary act.

My work on the case consisted primarily of traveling around the Navajo reservation in the company of Thomas Benally, our Navajo interpreter, tracking down people who had been alive in 1934 and whose memories were intact and relatively precise. We circumnavigated Hopiland, working from Tuba City on the west, to Teas Toh on the south, to Cottonwood on the east, to Shonto and Navajo Mountain on the north. (Shonto, one of my favorite Navajo place names, means "Sun on Water"; Oljeto, located nearby, "Moon on Water.")

Working with Thomas was, in itself, stimulating, enlightening, and, at odd times, frustrating. A graduate of Northern Arizona University in Flagstaff, he possessed an encyclopedic knowledge—both textbook and practical—of Navajo culture and history, and he had forsaken further schooling to help in the land dispute case. As a young man, however, and much to his parents' dismay, he had married a Hopi woman. Although he and his wife were divorced by the time I knew him, Thomas talked about their getting back together after the lawsuit was concluded, and I sometimes picked him up at her house in Flagstaff, where I also met their children. Several times I asked Thomas if his work on the case caused problems at home, and he quickly answered no. I believed him, or wanted to, but I also knew that his mood was tied closely to his relationship with his former wife and that his occasional binges usually followed fights with her.

Our method of work quickly became routine. We obtained lists of senior citizens from the chapter houses, the local governing units of the Navajo Nation, and set about locating the people. That part of the project entailed driving hundreds of miles over the unmarked, dirt back roads of the reservation, stopping to ask neighbors if they knew, for example, where Edith Salt Singer, John Bluesalt, George Littlesalt, or Curly Salt (all siblings, all in their eighties, all still residing within ten miles of each other) lived. Once we had located the person's hogan, I waited in the truck while Thomas knocked on the door and explained why we had come. After they learned what we were doing, most were willing to talk to us—they had heard about the land dispute and wanted to help their people. We then entered the hogan, sat on folding chairs or the sides of beds, and began the interview. Because most of the informants didn't speak English, Thomas translated my questions into Navajo and their answers into English as the two of us frantically scribbled notes.

We first asked to look at their Indian census cards, which contained reasonably accurate information about the person's birth date and the birth dates of his or her spouse and children. We then began to question them about the events of 1934, referring to that time as "the year when your first daughter was born" or "the year when the men came and killed the sheep and goats." (In 1934 the federal government, in an effort to rehabilitate the rangeland on the reservation, enforced mandatory livestock reduction against the Navajos, with the government agents often shooting the animals and burning the carcasses in front of the People's eyes. For the women especially—livestock belonging to the women in Navajo culture—that event was scratched indelibly on their memories. Fifty-five years later many of them cried and their voices shook as they recalled it. "Even if they take everything else," one woman said bitterly, "you won't starve if you have your sheep.") We asked where they were living in 1934, and with whom, and what they were doing. We asked if they saw any Hopis near their homes. If so, what were the Hopis doing—living, visiting, trading, hunting, trapping eagles? If a person's memory was good, the interview might last three hours; if bad, thirty minutes.

All of the people we interviewed had survived hard years on the reservation and had spent much of their lives outdoors; their faces were deeply lined and weathered, their eyes pale and rheumy, their hands (when I shook them) calloused. Most wore their hair long, the women typically gathering it into a bun, the men braiding it into a ponytail. Just as their mental capacities varied, so did their physical conditions. Some were so frail that they could only lie in bed as we talked (and those people, we knew, would not survive another winter), while others were still so strong and active that we needed to catch them early in the morning, before they left to herd their sheep for the day, or early in the evening, after they had returned home. (In general, the women fared better than the men, both physically and mentally. A majority of the people we recommended as witnesses were women.)

Most of our informants lived in traditional hogans —one-roomed circular or octagonal structures with dirt floors and split-juniper-and-clay roofs, their doors facing to the southeast, toward the sunrise. Of the dozens I visited, none had electricity or running water. We interviewed through the fall and winter, and a wood-burning stove often crackled softly in the middle of the room. Crowding the interior walls were the mean necessities of the people's lives: plastic containers of drinking water and cardboard boxes of food; caches of piñon and juniper wood; linoleum-topped tables, canvas cots, and metal-framed beds; piles of sateen skirts and denim jeans. All smelled alike, a faint but distinctive odor which I could never identify positively but which hinted of juniper smoke, human sweat, sheep's wool, and fine dust, an odor so elemental and somehow so familiar that it evoked in me a vague, powerful memory.

I will always remember some of those stories, but none so vividly as that of Dorothy Thompson, who, I am told, still lives near Shonto, Arizona, on the mesa below Navajo National Monument. Her appearance was unexceptional—just a short, matronly Navajo woman dressed in velveteen blouse and pleated skirt—but her manner was direct and her eyes, framed by wire-rimmed glasses, shone with intelligence. Although she preferred to speak Navajo, she understood English and sometimes began answering my questions even before Thomas translated them. At first I didn't believe that she could be as old as she said she was, but her census card showed her birth date as 1915 and her story—an archetypal story of life and death on the reservation—confirmed it.

She was born, Dorothy said, before the winter when so many of the People died. (In the winter of 1918–19 the worldwide flu epidemic killed, by conservative estimates, 10 percent of the Navajo population.) She grew up in her family's camp on Paiute Mesa near the Utah state line, north of where she lives today, spending her summers at her family's fields deep in Paiute Canyon. As a girl she heard stories of the "time of fearing," when her mother had been her age and when the Navajos, recently returned to the Four Corners area from their internment at Fort Sumner in eastern New Mexico, were being preyed upon by the Utes and Paiutes. At that time the People lived in fear of death and abduction, and the world seemed a hostile place. By the time Dorothy was born, those fears had subsided, but others soon replaced them.

Dorothy married her husband, Louis, in the late 1920s, and, as is Navajo custom, he moved in with her. The couple soon adopted a pattern of traveling seasonally between her parents' camp and her husband's parents' camp, nearer the national monument. They herded their sheep and goats along the mesas and farmed a small plot of land in Tsegi Canyon, on the trail to Keet Seel.

In the fall of 1934, when Dorothy was pregnant with their second child, Louis heard about wage work at Navajo Mountain, building small stone hogans to serve as dormitories for a new school. They had no truck or wagon, so Dorothy and Louis, carrying their infant daughter in a cradle board, left home and walked around the head of Paiute Canyon, onto the Rainbow Plateau, and across the Utah state line to Navajo Mountain, a distance of about fifty miles. En route they detoured to Shonto with their sheep and goats to have them branded and "dipped," i.e., disinfected for lice and scabies. They camped at Navajo Mountain for most of the fall, Louis working on the school and later on a WPA road project and Dorothy caring for their daughter and tending their flock.

Those were hard days, Dorothy said, when bad things were happening to the Navajo people. John Collier, the Commissioner of Indian Affairs, had promised them a better life if they would do as he said, if they would adopt white ways, but nothing came of those promises. Sickness was common, and there was never enough to eat. Dorothy remembered the Presbyterian nurse who lived in a canvas tent and ran a small clinic at Navajo Mountain during those years, and with a faint smile she recognized the name of the former trader at Navajo Mountain Trading Post, then (as now) one of the most isolated on the reservation. When the wage work ended around Thanksgiving, the young family walked toward home, herding their flock ahead of them and arriving in Shonto as the government agents were rounding up the livestock for reduction. The men killed most of their sheep and goats.

As she told me her story, Dorothy didn't cry and she didn't look at me in an accusatory fashion. She spoke slowly and in a controlled voice, sometimes looking at the ground for a minute before answering my questions, trying hard to remember. So much has happened, she said, so many people come and gone. She was sorry, she said, that she couldn't remember better.

Since that long-ago time she and Louis had done well for themselves, all things considered. Although their first daughter died in a whooping cough epidemic during the winter of 1934–35, their first son was born that January, and six other children followed. All but one live in the area today. Her daughter Helen runs the horse concession at the national monument and, coincidentally, is married to Clarence Austin. When we found Dorothy and Louis on a bright September afternoon, they were just leaving for Kayenta in their truck, but they deferred their trip to talk to us, sat with Thomas and me for more than three hours in the shade of a piñon tree outside of their hogan, shared with us their story of a small part of the Navajo reservation in 1934, a story told with understated eloquence and remarkable precision, a story of a world past, a world with a tenuous connection to the present in the form of two people's memories, a connection that someday soon will be broken forever.

Eventually I left my job in Arizona, returning home to New Mexico to work for the U.S. Department of the Interior in Santa Fe. I still work in Indian affairs, though no longer with the Navajos. I deal mostly with the New Mexican Pueblos, outwardly a more genial people. My contacts are cordial and polite. But sometimes, sitting in a meeting around a conference table, I think back to those distant evenings on the Navajo reservation, talking to Clarence Austin beside the hogan at Keet Seel or driving to Tuba City or Kayenta with Thomas Benally after a day of interviews, laughing at some stupid joke or discussing where to eat dinner—knowing that, for an instant, magically, we had reached through the glass pane between our two worlds.

Dog Canyon

I leave Lincoln on a clear, cool October morning, driving east along the Rio Bonito and Rio Hondo through tawny, sere foothills, the featureless plains of southeastern New Mexico opening ahead. At Roswell I turn south on U.S. 285 and begin tracking the Pecos River through an abused, barren landscape. Here the ground is dry and cracked, dust devils swirl across the highway, and cattle chew listlessly at bunchesgrasses under the barbed-wire fences. Solitary, sun-bleached mobile homes impart a forlorn aspect to the scene, and for long stretches the highway runs straight and flat, making a beeline for nowhere. ("Hardscrabble," Emmett said to me once, describing this area. "Like Oklahoma in the Dust Bowl days.") I pass the turnoff to Hagerman, the town proud of its reputation as the pit bull capital of New Mexico, and pass through Artesia, its small refinery closed this bright Sunday morning. Finally, twelve miles north of Carlsbad, across from the desolate shoreline of Brantley Reservoir, I turn west on New Mexico 137 and a sign announces, "Guadalupe Mountains National Park / Dog Canyon Ranger Station / 53 miles."

Along this rolling, two-laned macadam road the landscape appears less disturbed, less traumatized. Mesquite and creosote crowd the pavement, large-padded prickly pear cacti sprout on small ledges, and in Rocky Arroyo distinctly bedded white limestone cliffs rise above neat modern ranch houses, their lawns irrigated from a flowing stream. The road follows the stream through its cut in the mesa, then veers to the south, crossing an uninhabited expanse of Chihuahuan desert before climbing into the thick piñon-juniper growth of Lincoln National Forest. With each mile from the turnoff its condition deteriorates. I pass through the hamlet of Queen (where some optimistic local real estate mogul is attempting to sell vacation lots) and, finally, crawl down unpaved, rocky switchbacks into Dog Canyon. Along the east side of the canyon immense limestone cliffs run south into Texas. Through El Paso Gap, up the canyon, past the Hughes and Magby ranches, I head to the state line and park boundary.

I cross into the park, where the native grasses are once again growing waist high, and nod to Emmett, sitting in his truck in front of the tiny ranger station, guarding his home like an eagle its aerie. Some things never change, thank goodness. I pull into the parking area across from the campground. Just as I'm climbing out of the car, Emmett drives up and stops, and I walk around to his side of the truck. Although I haven't seen him in eleven years, he appears the same old Emmett: his cheeks flushed and ruddy, his Park Service parka zipped tight around his neck, his Stetson on his head. (From the neck up he has always reminded me of the Tin Man in *The Wizard of Oz.*) He doesn't give any indication he remembers me.

"Plannin' to camp?" he asks with a slight, home-spun drawl, his voice leisurely and apparently unconcerned (though I know better).

Yes, I say, for a couple of nights.

"I noticed your car is sorta loaded down. I thought you might be campin'. You can pitch your tent anywhere up from the bathrooms. Gonna be doing some hikin'?"

I say maybe, and he proceeds to orient me to the trails and to inform me of regulations and potential dangers, the latter being primarily rattlesnakes. All this time he is looking me over, assessing whether I'm what he used to call, in a different era, a "flea-bitten hippie" or, on the other hand, a responsible visitor. By the time he leaves, I can sense he is still undecided.

After pitching my tent, I walk up the arroyo under cover of red-leafed maples, sepia-toned oaks, olive-branched junipers, and smooth, red-barked madrones. Leaves crunch underfoot, and softball-sized spalls of whitish limestone, their corners rounded during their tumble from the high country, form a mosaic on the streambed. Although the sun is still shining brightly, it is low in the sky, the wind has come up, and the temperature is beginning to drop.

The escarpments and ridges forming the Guadalupes emerge from the low-lying desert in southeastern New Mexico and rise and converge to an apex, a prow, a few miles south of the Texas state line. Although the Guadalupes are not especially high mountains—Guadalupe Peak, the highest point in the range and in Texas, is 8,751 feet—south of the state line they loom nearly a vertical mile above the surrounding playas and salt flats.

The Guadalupes are composed of fossil-rich limestone and are a remnant of an ancient barrier reef that once encircled a large part of West Texas. In the words of Wallace Pratt, a prominent geologist and oil man who donated the first tract of land for the park, the Guadalupes "in their entirety are no more than a profoundly uplifted segment of Capitan barrier reef—a wall or ridge of rock built by lowly marine organisms in warm, shallow, clear waters on the floor of a long-vanished sea."

Guadalupe Mountains National Park was opened to the public in 1972. By the time I worked here in 1979, Emmett was already the park veteran, having moved down from Carlsbad Caverns in 1964, shortly after Mr. Pratt donated his land to the federal government. During the park's early years he was the chief ranger in the more heavily visited Pine Springs District, along the highway on the southeast side of the mountains. But he didn't like dealing with the increasing numbers of tourists stopping at the new park, and shortly after my time here he transferred to Dog Canyon, which is far enough off the beaten track to discourage casual visitors.

Emmett is not the kind of chipper, friendly ranger the Park Service likes to have greeting visitors to our national treasures. He has always been prone to pigeon-hole people on the basis of their appearance and to treat them accordingly (e.g., flea-bitten hippies), and he is one of the more profane people I have known.

Thinking back, I recall one moment in particu-lar that captures both of those propensities. During the time I worked here, Emmett hired a new seasonal employee sight-unseen, based only on an application that showed the man to be a native West Texan, a grad-uate of Texas Tech, and skilled with horses and other pack animals. When Blake reported for work, however, he was not the slim-hipped, soft-spoken, crew-cut cow-boy Emmett obviously had envisioned; rather, he was gregarious, talkative, and flamboyant looking, sporting long, uncombed flame-red hair and a silver earring in his left lobe. After Emmett met Blake for the first time, my boss asked him what he thought of his new employee. Emmett mulled the question for a minute, then offered his appraisal:

"Blake seems like a pretty nice fella," he allowed, "but what the fuck with that earring?"

I also recall a day when Emmett walked into the crowded visitor center fiddling with a retractable tape measure he had used to measure skid marks at the scene of an accident on the highway. The tape wouldn't wind back into its case.

"Goddam fuckin' tinker toy," he said to me in his normal speaking voice, oblivious to the other people standing nearby. "The government buys this cheap shit and it breaks the first time you use it, and then the government replaces it with more cheap shit." He shook his head and chuckled. "No wonder we're all goin' broke."

I never found Emmett's profanity offensive, partly because it seemed a natural, unstressed part of his speech, his patois, his adopted West Texas tongue; and partly because it was, on his part, so far as I could tell, completely unconscious. He did not intend to shock or offend. By the same token, he lacked the awareness to censor his own speech. He talked in the same manner to everyone. The secretaries in the town office blanched and scurried for cover when he walked through the door, and I suspect the Park Service muck-amucks were relieved when he requested his transfer to Dog Canyon.

As I return to the campground, Emmett drives up again and stops—I'm the only camper here, and the upper end of Dog Canyon is not large—and we begin to chat. I tell him I worked in the park a long time ago, and he cocks his head and studies me out of the sides of his eyes from behind his thick glasses. I still don't see any sign of recognition, but he smiles and chuckles, and we talk for a few minutes about former coworkers, now all long gone from Guadalupe. After we exhaust that topic, I ask him how the larger predators in the park—the black bears and mountain lions—are faring.

"Oh, I suppose they're holdin' their own," he says after considering the question for a minute. "They just have a hard time survivin' in such a small area. And if they roam outside the park . . . well, you know, the ranch element just blows 'em away.

"Black bears are protected animals in Texas now, but mountain lions aren't—it's just another varmint they can shoot anytime they want. Lions are protected in New Mexico, but, gee, they have huntin' season for 'em, and they get permits to trap 'em too. Wildlife just has a hard time today.

"These guys come around in their beautiful four-wheel-drives, with fancy binoculars and scopes on their rifles. What's the animal got? Four legs and maybe a good nose. So they're at a disadvantage. I'm sorry, but I just can't make those guys out to be big, macho, brave men. I tell some of 'em around here that the only effort they put into it is squeezing the goddam trigger—about a quarter-pound of pressure.

"I'm sure they don't toast to my health." He laughs, perhaps a bit too heartily, then suddenly grows quiet and pensive.

"When you're in country like this . . . Well, your outlook on wildlife is just different when you've been protectin' 'em your whole career." There is a note of sadness in his voice.

I am reminded of a famous Aldo Leopold essay titled "Thinking Like a Mountain." In that essay Leopold describes how, as a young man in the White Mountains of Arizona, callow and "full of trigger-itch," he shot and wounded an old wolf. He reached the animal "in time to watch a fierce green fire dying in her eyes"—a moment that affected Leopold deeply. Out of that moment he came to recognize the role of predators in the natural regulation of animal populations and the importance of them to the wild spirit of the world. Few hunters, however, attain such insights.

I ask Emmett about the ranchers immediately to the north of the boundary—the Hughes and Magby clans—who vehemently opposed the establishment of the park and, during the 1970s, refused to grant a right-of-way for the Dog Canyon access road. They continue to complain bitterly about depredations on their livestock by mountain lions who, they say, retreat into the sanctuary of the park after making the kills. In the last few years they have pressured their congressmen for permission to track the lions into the park to eliminate them once and for all. The dispute is long standing. When I worked here, the Dog Canyon ranger found a lion carcass draped across the park's boundary fence—a taunt from the neighbors to the north.

"They'd do anything for a goddam cow," Emmett says matter-of-factly. "You'd think it was the goddam Golden Calf."

He pauses for a minute, pondering. "I don't understand those people," he says then. "Their solution to every problem is to kill something. Blow it away. They think it's their birthright.

"Oh, they talk about how much they hate the federal government and all its regulations, but these days they make their living off the goddam BLM and government. Eliminate the federal government, and they'd starve."

I ask him how he gets along with them, his closest neighbors in this isolated country.

He shrugs. "I've always just made it a point to tend to my side of the fence and mind my own business."

He is quiet for a long while. "This canyon was named for the prairie dogs," he says finally, staring off through the windshield of his truck. "Used to be huge towns of 'em out there in the grasses. That was probably somethin' to see. I imagine you had your birds of prey swoopin' down to pick 'em up. But they killed all of them too. Killed everything for their goddam cattle."

At dusk, after my camp dinner, I stroll around the loop at road's end here in Dog Canyon. More deer than I have ever seen in the wild—fifty or sixty muleys—are browsing in the meadow around the road. As I walk closer, all of them stop, prick up their ears, and stare at me suspiciously. When I get too close, they begin to edge away slowly, still chewing but ready to bound if I make a false move.

I recall some favorite lines from Stephen Vincent Benét:

When Daniel Boone goes by, at night,
The phantom deer arise
And all lost, wild America
Is burning in their eyes.

I inspect the tidy barn and the official Park Service horse trailers at the end of the circle. Emmett loves horses, and when he patrols the high country, he still does so, as he always has, on horseback. (In the early days he bought saddles and tack with his own money and donated them to the park.) Out back of the barn, in the corral, three well-fed, recently brushed horses—a sorrel, a palomino, and a gray—are munching on hay in their feed bins. As I watch, a doe walks up daintily beside the palomino and tries to sneak some hay. The palomino noses her away, whinnying softly.

As I walk back to my campsite, the first owl of the evening hoots in the talus below the cliffs. The wind has calmed, and the night—a cold, breathless autumn night, the sky as black as obsidian—descends on the Dog.

In the morning the sun comes late to the campground in the canyon, finally peeking over the limestone cliffs long after dawn on the east side of the mountains. After a leisurely breakfast I load my day pack, register at the trailhead, and begin walking up the Tejas Trail. I walk by Lost Peak and into the high country, climbing through piñon, juniper, and scrub oak into ponderosa pine, Douglas fir, and limber pine. Despite the thick forest the wind on the ridges is gusty and swirling, reminding me, in case I had forgotten, that the winds here can be a relentless irritant and menace. In the Guadalupes one appreciates the fact that the wind, like little else in this world, can drive people mad.

The worst winds gather on the immense salt flats west of the park, converge at the southern tip of the mountains, and funnel ferociously through Guadalupe Pass. Dog Canyon, set between the Brokeoff Mountains to the west and the main body of the Guadalupes to the east and south, is relatively protected and calm. On the east side of the mountains, however, it is not uncommon for the winds to blow steadily for days at a time, forty or fifty miles per hour.

When the winds begin to howl, nothing—not people, not horses, not wildlife—likes to venture out. At the old visitor center, at the top of the pass, the wind shredded the flag every couple of weeks, and the official anemometer literally blew apart in a gust one day. Everyone who spends time in the Guadalupes develops a repertory of stories about the wind. The story of the two truck drivers pulling a double-wide mobile home who stopped one day at the Pine Springs Cafe along the highway on the southeast side of the mountains; while they were inside drinking coffee, a gust blew the double-wide, in Emmett's words, "to smithereens." The story of the pilot who claimed her single-engine plane was blown to a standstill one day as she tried to fly through the pass. (Not surprisingly, the mountains' southeastern escarpment is littered with the wreckage of other planes.)

For more than sixty-five years Walter and Bertha Glover ran the Pine Springs Cafe. When tourists asked Mrs. Glover if the wind always blew like this, she often responded with her favorite line.

"Oh no," she liked to say as she turned away slyly. "Sometimes it blows from the other direction."

Walking along this rocky trail, I also recall that the Guadalupes are the snakiest place I've ever hiked, a fact that causes me some apprehension this warm October day. Other places have snakes, but none I know has the variety and population density of the Guadalupes. Western diamondback, black-tailed, prairie, and rock— four species of rattlesnakes alone. (My reptile field guide provides this rather alarming information about the prairie rattler: "Western counterpart of the Timber Rattlesnake but much more excitable and aggressive. . . . [L]arge numbers may overwinter together at a common den site.") When I worked here and routinely patrolled the trails, I was always arousing furious, buzzing rattlers. I have nothing against our reptilian neighbors—live and let live, I say—but by the time the first snow fell, I was beginning to see sticks writhe and coil.

All in all, the Guadalupes are a tough place to live even today, and they would have been a much tougher place to eke out a living fifty or a hundred or two hundred years ago. Not many people tried: small bands of Comanches and Mescalero Apaches in temporary camps in the canyons, a few white settlers and ranchers around the base of the mountains. In recent years the Park Service employees have joined that lineage, but the isolation drives most of them away after a year or two. Now that Bertha Glover is gone, Emmett may have lived here—by "here" I don't mean the surrounding desert, which in many ways is more hospitable than the high country, but close in to the mountains themselves— longer than anybody.

He has always been something of an enigma to me. Although he mentioned once that he grew up on a farm in Missouri and served in the Marine Corps before starting to work for the Park Service, he rarely talks about his past, and it usually seems as if he had no life before he came to the Guadalupes. He takes his job seriously, giving it priority over everything else he does, and he expects the people who work for him to do the same. "Working for the Park Service is not an eight-to-five job," he likes to say, and he has no patience with coworkers who balk at working overtime (whether paid or not) or who complain about being called after hours for emergencies.

By modern standards his view of women is not enlightened. Depending on his mood, he tends to see them either in idealized terms, i.e., as members of a fairer, gentler sex, or as impediments to a man's doing his job. I once overheard him chastising a ranger who had been absent from the park during a search and rescue. "You can't work in this park," he said peevishly, "if you're always gonna be runnin' into town with your wife to buy a sack of potatoes."

In addition to being suspicious of people he meets and judgmental of people he knows, he is full of outrageous (though not necessarily unthoughtful) opinions about the larger issues of the day (e.g., his observation about the problem of illegal immigration from Mexico: "We wouldn't have this problem today if Sam Houston had marched to Mexico City a hundred and fifty years ago and kicked their asses. We'd just have a few more states, and probably everyone would be better off."). But in his own curmudgeonly way Emmett can be charming, and he is unfailingly honest and dependable. I like Emmett, much more than I like the glib, overly familiar people who seem to greet me everywhere these days, and there is no one I would rather have caretaking a remote, rugged, beautiful place like Dog Canyon.

During my time at the park I didn't work in Emmett's division. Although I often saw him in the visitor center and on the roads and occasionally visited him in the historic Rader ranch house where he lived then, I spent only one full workday with him, a day when I was assigned to accompany him to the west side of the park to help him repair part of the boundary fence that had been reported damaged, a day that remains my most vivid memory of my months in the Guadalupes.

I met him at the visitor center early in the morning. Emmett is fair complected and, out of a fear of skin cancer, has developed a fanatical aversion to the sun. That day he was wearing his standard out-of-doors work uniform: a stylish beaver-felt Stetson, under which a red bandanna flowed down over his ears and the back of his neck; dark glasses; zinc oxide on the bridge of his nose; another bandanna knotted around his neck, available, if necessary, to protect his chin; a long-sleeved khaki shirt and khaki pants (he rarely wore the standard Park Service gray-and-green); work boots; and leather gloves. By pulling up the knotted bandanna, he could ensure that not a single square inch of his skin was exposed. He looked like a spaceman in a 1950s sci-fi movie. I knew Emmett, and his outfit struck me as odd or amusing. I wondered what visitors who encountered him thought.

Before we left the Pine Springs area, we stopped at Mrs. Glover's store, where Emmett bought me a can of pop to drink on the way over. Mrs. Glover liked Emmett—together they shared the easy manners of West Texas locals. Mrs. Glover was the one from whom I had learned a surprising bit of information about Emmett's past: that he had been married once; but, in her words, "it didn't take."

After leaving Mrs. Glover's, we drove down the pass, around El Capitan (the prow of the Guadalupes), and west to the turnoff for Williams Ranch. We unlocked the gate and ground up the dirt road in four-wheel drive, the immense cliffs, talus slopes, and alluvial fans of the mountains' western prospect towering above us. Before we started to work on the fence, Emmett wanted to check on a couple of windmills he had repaired and got pumping again. He was keeping the old stock tanks filled for the wildlife, and as we approached the first one, set in a small grove of cottonwoods near an abandoned ranch house, a golden eagle flew up suddenly from its perch in one of the trees and a coyote loped off into the brush, glancing at us over its shoulder. After we got out of the truck, we heard songbirds in the trees, but otherwise the day was quiet and still. A benign morning in the Guadalupes. Emmett was excited by the wildlife we had seen.

"It's starting to come back," he said, "after having been shot at and blown away all these years."

He got his binoculars from the back of the truck and scanned the desert in the direction of the mountains. He was a man in his element.

After checking the water level in the tanks, we drove farther, parked, and walked up an arroyo toward the damaged fence. There, in the arroyo, we came upon a scatter of owl pellets and, above our heads, high in the wall of the arroyo, the burrow of a great horned owl. We spent twenty or thirty minutes examining and collecting pellets, which Emmett said he was going to take back to the visitor center in case someone wanted to use them in an interpretive exhibit. Each pellet contained dozens of rodent bones—femurs, vertebrae, and fragments of skull—in a matrix of hair and fur, and each told a story of a vigilant watch and silent, swooping wings; a brief, futile struggle; and a small, noiseless death in the night.

We spent four or five hours on the west side, not talking much, just restringing barbed wire and occasionally stopping to identify a bird, eat our brown-bag lunches, and watch the shadows shift on the limestone escarpment. At day's end Emmett didn't thank me for helping him—he didn't believe in thanking people for doing what they were paid to do—but I could tell he was pleased with our work, and when we got back to Pine Springs, he hurried into the visitor center like a little boy to show everyone the treasures we had found.

The story has an addendum and, perhaps, a moral, though it still is not clear to me what that moral properly is. The year after Emmett and I worked on the west side, the Park Service natural resources specialists heard about his stock tanks and ordered them drained. The tanks were not a part of the natural ecosystem, they said, and therefore did not belong in a national park, where the restoration of the ecosystem is one of the primary goals.

I don't know what Emmett thought about their decision. It is tempting to picture him as the defender of wildlife battling the narrow-minded, technical bureaucrats and to assume that he disagreed with what they did, but Emmett, aware of the larger mission of the Park Service, may have appreciated the rationale behind their decision. He may have thought to himself, "I suppose we mustn't alter the environment, even to favor the animals, even to compensate for their decimation during the past century. I suppose they're right." He may have thought that. If, indeed, they were right.

Now, eleven years later, he is still here, and everyone else involved in that particular incident is long gone. He outlasted all of them. And as I descend from Manzanita Ridge into Dog Canyon this warm, breezy October afternoon, I find myself wondering if, after all, he can help himself; wondering if, hidden in these dry foothills, there are other products of his initiative: seeps dug out under limestone ledges, check dams pooling rocky arroyos, wooden troughs filled with spring water.

In the middle of the night I awake to the sound of an animal snuffling near the tent. I fumble for my flashlight, sit up, and shine it out the front door. A ringtail cat, tail as long as its slender body, is nosing around the picnic table at my campsite. Its movements appear routine, its behavior tame, but when it looks in my direction, its eyes suddenly burn green and wild in the beam of light.

I awake early, struggle into my clothes, and crawl out of the tent into the dawn chill. Above me, in the brushy talus below the cliffs, I suddenly hear, like a bow pulled across a violin, the call of a bull elk. I scan the slopes for ten minutes but am unable to spot the animal.

The indigenous elk were exterminated by the early settlers, but a replacement species was introduced in 1929. Although the herd is not growing in size, it is sustaining itself and the animals now contribute their awkward, eerie presence to the canyon.

I drink hot tea and fiddle with my breakfast until the sun clears the cliffs, then slowly fold the tent and pack the car. On my way out of the park I stop at Emmett's house—a neat, new frame house—to say good-bye and thank him for taking care of the place. He comes to the door in his khakis.

"How was your walk yesterday?" he asks.

Pleasant but windy, I respond.

"Did you see any wildlife up there?"

When I say no, he looks disappointed. On the wall behind him a mountain lion stares at me from a picture frame, its ears erect, its eyes penetrating and impassive.

I take my leave and drive slowly out of the park, past the Hughes and Magby ranches, down Dog Canyon, and through El Paso Gap. I waited eleven years to come back to this place, and I may not return for many more—

my life is taking me in other directions these days. But Emmett—once again, as always, he stays. He has devoted his life to the protection of these lonely canyons and mountains, and he knows them better than anybody. What a curious, solitary character he is. Why is he still here? What does this place mean to him? And what did he leave behind?

As I climb the rocky switchbacks out of Dog Canyon, I realize I will never know the answers to those questions. Nor, I suppose, do I need to. It is enough, isn't it, that he has stayed and knows? Enough that he is the dog in the Dog, the keeper of the kingdom, the last lone ranger.

The Adobe Plains

Today I-25 follows the route of the Santa Fe Trail east from the city of Santa Fe, through the mesa-rimmed foothills of the Sangre de Cristo Mountains and along the Pecos River, before bending north and emerging from the foothills near Las Vegas, New Mexico. Between Las Vegas and the town of Wagon Mound, a distance of forty miles, the modern highway continues to shadow the old trail, the mountains now forming a rampart to the west, the high plains of New Mexico—the adobe plains—stretching away to the east.

On a cool January day, with high cirrus clouds filtering the sunlight, I leave the interstate at Wagon Mound and drive east on New Mexico 120. Wagon Mound—the long, low mesa itself, the landmark that to early travelers resembled oxen pulling a wagon—rises to the south of the highway, its small volcanic scarp capping a talus of lichen-covered boulders, sepia-toned scrub oaks, and patches of snow in deep shadow. Ahead the landscape opens to the horizon, a seemingly endless expanse of tawny, windswept grasses and shallow caprock canyons.

The highway is empty, and I slow the car and relax my grip on the steering wheel. Winter suits this country, I find myself thinking, because the signs of winter—pale sunlight, bitter winds, rustling grasses—accentuate its austere, heartrending essence. "Loneliness is an aspect of the land," Scott Momaday wrote of a similar landscape in western Oklahoma. "All things in the plain are isolate; there is no confusion of objects in the eye, but *one* hill or *one* tree or *one* man." Yes, this is a lonely landscape—an anthropomorphic characterization, perhaps, but accurate nonetheless.

Driving along this deserted highway, however, I also feel a strange, euphoric giddiness—a prickling in my guts, a lightness in my head. This spacious landscape inspires an irrational feeling of freedom. A man or woman still may walk unimpeded over much of this land, still may walk for days or weeks or months without interruption or effort, or so it seems.

Many writers have likened the plains to the ocean because of the broad, featureless vistas common to both. In *Commerce of the Prairies* Josiah Gregg, the early chronicler of the Santa Fe Trail, described the landscape through which he passed as "the grand 'prairie ocean.'" "Not a single landmark is to be seen for more than forty miles," he wrote, "scarcely a visible eminence by which to direct one's course. All is as level as the sea, and the compass [is] our surest, as well as principal guide." Gregg, fond of the comparison, went so far as to suggest that a system of maritime law should control among traders on the prairie.

But because the ocean has always inspired in me dread, not exhilaration, I find the comparison imperfect. The ocean is (and always will be) a world foreign and frightening to a terrestrial animal, rendering impossible our natural locomotion and concealing in its murky depths hideous creatures that otherwise appear to us only in nightmares. The ocean seems a weighty, disabling medium, one that threatens our very breath. But the plains—that world beckons us; there is a lightness in its air, a lightness even in the word itself.

The highway descends gradually toward the Canadian River canyon along a broad, grassy swale. The canyon, six hundred vertical feet from rimrock to river, was a substantial obstacle to people traveling on horse-back or by wagon, and the Santa Fe Trail avoided it by crossing the Canadian to the north, near what is now the town of Springer. The canyon's sandstone rim supports a thick piñon-juniper forest and harbors small stands of ponderosa pines, recalling canyons on the Colorado Plateau far to the west. At the river itself, choked with tamarisk, I cross into Harding County, the least popu-lous in New Mexico—2,122 square miles in extent, home to one thousand souls.

East of the canyon the highway approaches the small, disintegrating town of Roy, whose community water tower features an orange Texas longhorn, the mas-cot of the high school sports teams. More than anything else, this part of New Mexico (once claimed by Texas, ceded to the United States in 1850) is cattle country. An empty holding pen sits beside the highway, and as I walk around the small, moribund downtown, two or three trucks pulling ventilated trailers rattle through, leaving in their wakes the rich smells of livestock and manure.

Some of the buildings in Roy are of typical New Mexican construction—flat-roofed adobe or stucco—but there are pitched-roofed frame houses as well, and the Baptist Church, built in 1894, looks positively midwestern. A white, gabled building with leaded windows, capped by a clapboard-and-shingle steeple. The names of the ranchers in the area tell the same story: Ray, Mahoney, Ivey, Mitchell, Hicks. This is the part of New Mexico where the Spanish and Mexican influence wanes and the Anglo influence waxes. This is where settlers from the east found short-grass prairies unoccupied except by nomadic Indians. This is where they homesteaded ranches and imported livestock and where their grandchildren and great-grandchildren live today.

That is not to say that Hispanics have never ventured onto the plains. Coronado passed through here in 1540, returning to Mexico from his fruitless quest for Quivira's riches (having been deliberately misguided by the Indian known to him as the Turk), and Gregg describes meeting a solitary *Cibolero* or Mexican buffalo hunter. (Gregg reports that these "hardy devotees of the chase" usually wore "leathern trousers and jackets, and flat straw hats" and dangled tassels of "gay parti-colored stuffs" from their scabbards and muskets.) And Hispanics long have infiltrated the dominant Anglo culture of this part of the state—Harding County now is more than 40 percent Hispanic—though, as elsewhere, they tend to hold menial jobs and lack political voice.

From Roy I drive northeast to Chicosa Lake State Park. A regular stop on the Goodnight and Loving cattle trail from Fort Worth to Denver, Chicosa Lake was a dependable source of water in an otherwise arid stretch of country. Charles Goodnight and Oliver Loving pioneered their trail across West Texas and up the Pecos River in the years after the Civil War. They sold cattle to the U.S. Army at Fort Sumner and Fort Union in New Mexico before continuing north to the lucrative Colorado markets. The risks were substantial: trackless plains (particularly the Llano Estacado), unpredictable weather, hostile Indians.

On only their second drive Loving and One-Armed Bill Wilson, a hired hand, rode ahead of the herd toward Santa Fe to bid on army cattle contracts. In southern New Mexico, just east of the Guadalupe Mountains, they encountered a large band of Comanches, who chased the two men to the banks of the Pecos and pinned them down with rifles, bows and arrows, and rocks. A bullet shattered Loving's wrist. That night, at Loving's command, Wilson swam downstream, edging past a Comanche guard, and began walking the eighty miles back to the herd. After holding the Indians at bay for two days, Loving escaped upstream, encountered three Mexicans and a German boy in a wagon, and hired them to take him to Fort Sumner. There, for a time, he seemed to be recovering. But his wound suddenly worsened. Gangrene set in, and his arm was amputated. He died twenty-two days later.

On his death bed Loving told Goodnight, "I regret to have to be laid away in a foreign country."

Goodnight promised to bury him at home, in Weatherford, Texas, near Fort Worth. The next spring he exhumed Loving's body and did so, carrying it 450 miles in a wagon drawn by six mules, accompanied by a cortege of cowboys. (Goodnight and Loving undoubtedly were the prototypes for the characters Call and McCrae in *Lonesome Dove*.) Goodnight lived to age ninety-three, establishing himself as one of the most prominent (and, in his old age, cantankerous) cattlemen in the Texas panhandle. Such is the stuff of which legends rightfully are made.

This cool January day, however, Chicosa Lake shows little sign of its fabled past. It is only a dry, shallow depression in the ground, its bed caked with alkaline deposits, the grasses on its shoreline raked by the restless wind.

I continue up New Mexico 120, passing into Union County and fording the shallow winter flow of Ute Creek, heading toward Clayton. Cattle graze in dumb contentment in the immense grasslands (not pastures, but fenced range). Although we may imagine that the plains appear today as they did to the first settlers, in reality they have been subtly and irrevocably altered. The introduction of millions of head of cattle and intensive grazing over the course of a century have devastated many of the native grasses—notably little bluestem (*Andropogon scoparius*) and the various species of grama (*Bouteloua* sp.)—and compacted the topsoil, impairing its ability to absorb and retain water. As a result, runoff has increased and arroyos have downcut dramatically, intersecting, draining, and lowering the water table. Extensive pumping of groundwater has lowered it even more. (Either may have caused the dewatering of Chicosa Lake.) In recent years dust storms, always bad, have worsened.

Still, the plains have retained their essential majesty. The changes in the ecosystem, though profound, have not destroyed the landscape's visual appeal. Today, as always, what strikes one first about this country is its vastness of scale—the astonishing appearance of faraway objects across an expanse of open earth. This afternoon, for example, off to the north, forty miles distant, I can see volcanic remnants in the area around Sierra Grande and Capulin, their conical shapes shimmering on the horizon.

Like others, Gregg commented on the clarity of the air on the plains and, paradoxically, on the ways in which the clear air can trick the eye. "The optical illusions occasioned by the rarefied and transparent atmosphere of these elevated plains," he wrote, "are truly remarkable, affording another example of its purity. One would almost fancy himself looking through a spy-glass, for objects frequently appear at scarce one-fourth of their real distance—frequently much magnified, and more especially elevated." Gregg also speculated at length on the optics of mirages, which he called "false ponds."

▼ The Adobe Plains ▼

As I turn onto U.S. 56, I tune in the Clayton AM radio station. The program is country and western, interrupted only by the network news—dominated by grim dispatches from the Persian Gulf—and the local calendar and weather. Children's story hour at the public library has been canceled this week. AA and Narcotics Anonymous will meet at the town hall as usual. A cold air mass is spreading south from Canada. Snow and increasing winds are forecast. By morning arctic air will have invaded the adobe plains.

After checking into the Holiday Motel, conveniently located near the Union County Feed Lot, across the railroad overpass on the northwest side of Clayton, I drive back into town to eat dinner at the Eklund Hotel Restaurant and Saloon. Outside, the Eklund appears a boxy, nondescript sandstone building. Inside, it is a vintage Old West eatery, with carved plaster ceilings; amber-glass chandeliers; golden, floral-patterned wallpaper; and soft-cushioned, velvet-upholstered chairs—the decadent, musty legacy of what was once a grand hotel on the frontier. The menu informs me that in its heyday, after the Colorado and Southern Railroad had been completed and Clayton had established itself as a major cattle shipping point, the Eklund was the "only first-class hotel between Fort Worth and Denver."

The clientele is mostly local and white, with the men dressed in polished boots, cattleman's jeans, and snap-button shirts. A few are wearing ties for their Saturday night dinners. As I wait for my meal, a local family—parents and adult daughter—sits down at the table across from mine. The man wears business clothes minus a tie; perhaps he is the local banker. The mother and daughter are dressed alike in slacks and prim, high-collared blouses; they appear demure, but their gaze is hard and calculating.

Their conversation takes in the other people in the dining room, most of whom they know. They recognize that the only Hispanic family is celebrating the birthday of one of its daughters, a current star on Clayton High's formidable girls' basketball team. They speculate on her age, their voices edged with condescension.

As other families leave, they stop by my neighbors' table to chat and pay their respects. The talk is cordial and meaningless. Most glance at me with idle curiosity, and I sense their bottom line: a single white male, decently dressed, longish hair; an out-of-towner, passing through, nothing to worry about.

After finishing my meal, I wander into the Eklund Saloon, where I am disappointed to find that customers may no longer sit at the original mahogany bar but must be served at tables or booths. The room is crowded with skiers returning home to Texas from Taos and Colorado, and the mood is festive. Everyone ignores the framed photographs and newspaper reprints on the wall, the documentation of Black Jack Ketchum's life and gruesome death.

Although the details of Ketchum's story vary with the telling, a common legend emerges. It is, until the end, a tale fit for Hollywood, and it goes something

like this: During the 1890s Ketchum led an outlaw gang
that operated in New Mexico's Boot Heel and southeastern Arizona, mostly robbing trains and stagecoaches. On
one occasion they engaged in a bloody shootout with a
posse in which several members of the gang were killed.
Around the turn of the century Ketchum moved to
northeastern New Mexico, where in April 1901 he tried
single-handedly to rob the Colorado and Southern train
at Twin Butte Curve, between Folsom and Des Moines.
After he stopped the train, however, the conductor shot-
gunned him at close range, nearly severing his right arm
and knocking him to the ground. The next morning a
badly bleeding Ketchum surrendered to railroad agents
or a posse. He was taken by train to Trinidad, Colorado,
where his arm was amputated, and to Santa Fe, where he
was tried, convicted, and sentenced to hang. He then was
transferred to Clayton for his execution.

On the gallows, according to the legend, an
impatient Ketchum told the nervous hangman, "Hurry
it up—I'm due in hell for dinner." True to his contrary
nature he requested that he be buried face down.

The good people of Clayton gathered on April 26
to watch the outlaw die. Some brought picnics. The inex-
perienced hangman, however, botched the execution. The
noose was not coiled or fitted properly, or there was too
much slack in the rope. Black Jack was not hanged but
decapitated. His severed head rolled into the crowd. His
body jerked spasmodically on the ground. The doctor
assigned to the execution, not knowing what else to do,
listened for a heartbeat and certified that Ketchum was

dead. One of the photographs displayed in the Eklund Saloon shows the doctor and sheriff kneeling glumly beside the body, a bloody stump where its head used to be.

After leaving the Eklund, I cruise through downtown Clayton. The temperature is dropping, and the wind has begun to howl. The electronic billboard at the Farmers and Stockmens Bank reports 28° F at 8:11 PM.

Clayton is a western town, with wide main streets and a single stoplight at its major intersection. These days the streets are uncrowded, and half of the downtown stores are vacant. Although Clayton's economic mainstay is cattle, the town enjoyed a boom a decade ago when carbon dioxide from the Bravo Dome field was being piped to the Permian Basin in West Texas for secondary oil recovery. Then the oil market went bust, taking with it a chunk of Clayton's economy. In the last five years the town's population has dwindled.

Still, Clayton is hanging on. Doing better than many small towns in rural New Mexico. The cattle business is steady. The railroad helps, as does the convergence of three U.S. highways. Tourists driving to the mountains of New Mexico and Colorado support a handful of gas stations, motels, and restaurants. Things could be worse.

This cold Saturday night in January Clayton slumbers. A few trucks are parked outside the Country Tavern and the Roadrunner Lounge. Otherwise the streets are deserted. The railroad tracks are quiet. The wind howls, carrying the smell of the feed lot across the town.

The next morning I go for breakfast at the Rabbit Ear Cafe, located on the town side of the railroad tracks. Although the cafe's interior is old and plain, the linoleum table tops are spotless and the aluminum surfaces behind the counter shine from years of polishing.

The waitress, a middle-aged Hispanic woman, brings me a menu and takes my order, and an older Hispanic man—probably her father or father-in-law—cooks in back. The cafe is empty except for the booth two down from mine, occupied by three Hispanic men dressed in jeans, work shirts, and baseball caps. Over cups of coffee they talk quietly, discussing the war and then, in a brighter tone, the most recent victory of the Clayton High girls' basketball team. When the waitress stops to listen, the man closest to her reaches out his arm and gently touches her lower back. The men's conversation passes from English into Spanish and back again. It is an effortless weaving together of the two tongues, a soft, bilingual murmuring, an early-morning, working-class benediction.

After breakfast I drive out of town toward Clayton Lake State Park, passing the Five State Livestock Auction Company (the five states being New Mexico, Texas, Oklahoma, Colorado, and Kansas) and climbing onto the shoulder of Rabbit Ear Mountain. Although Rabbit Ear rises only a thousand feet above Clayton, it is visible for many miles across the plains and was an important landmark on the Cimarron Cutoff of the Santa Fe Trail, whose route I rejoin this morning.

The view from Rabbit Ear is panoramic. To the west Sierra Grande rises in the distance, its flanks dusted with fresh snow. In all other directions the plains undulate and stretch to the horizon, their surface broken only by low mesas and shallow canyons.

Geographically this part of New Mexico belongs to the plains. Boise City, Oklahoma, is forty-four miles away; Elkhart, Kansas, forty miles beyond that. Dodge City is closer than Santa Fe. More importantly, since its settlement a century ago this area has participated in the livestock-based culture that marks the high plains from the Texas panhandle to Saskatchewan. The locals here feel more kinship with people in, say, Amarillo, or Goodland, Kansas, or Ogallala, Nebraska, than with those in Albuquerque. This morning the Clayton radio station announces that the girls' basketball team will travel to Colby, Kansas, later in the week, as it does every year, to play in a regional tournament.

Rabbit Ear Mountain was named, not for any fancied resemblance to a rabbit's ears, but for a Cheyenne Indian warrior whose ears were frostbitten and mangled and who, according to legend, was killed in battle and buried near one of the mountain's two prominences. For thousands of years this area was a part of Indian country. Prehistoric Indians hunted mammoths, bison, and giant ground sloths here, and in historic times it was a meeting ground, and battleground, for some of the greatest plains tribes. Comanches, Kiowas, Pawnees, Cheyennes, Arapahoes—all passed through here. Gregg reports a friendly encounter in this area with "a party of about eighty Sioux, who were on a tour upon the Prairies for the purpose of trading with, stealing from or marauding upon the south-western nations." He records a similar friendly encounter with a contingent of Blackfoot and Gros Ventres, also from far to the north, and his account is filled with tense meetings with large bands of local Indians.

At Clayton Lake State Park I take a short walk to look at the dinosaur tracks uncovered when material was excavated for the spillway of the small dam across Seneca Creek. If anything, the temperature has fallen since last night, and the wind has not abated, so I bundle up in winter coat, scarf, hat, and heavy gloves. Even so, my cheeks soon begin to tingle and burn with the cold.

As I walk, I find myself humming melancholy folk songs. That music, often inspired by similar lonely landscapes, captures the spirit of this place. "Four Strong Winds," by the Canadian Ian Tyson, for example. And a modern English folk song, whose lyrics include this verse:

> Winter has come, Annie,
> No strength in the sun, Annie,
> And when it's gone, Annie,
> Where shall we be?

Poignance—a piercing of the heart—and the prospect or memory of love's failure—those are the evocations of this landscape and season.

Most of Clayton Lake is frozen, and the only sounds this morning are the honking of a small flock of ducks as they wheel and land in a rippled cove and the twittering of chickadees as they hop and flutter in the grasses on the earthen dam. And the sound of the wind in the grasses. As always, the wind. My friend Randy grew up in nearby Des Moines, and the wind is the element, the force, the *thing* he associates most strongly with this area. When I told him I was coming out here and asked him what to do, he said to me, "Sit and listen to the wind— when it's blowing but not roaring in your ears. Sit and listen to the wind for an hour, and you will begin to hear the voices." The voices of the past, I think he meant, of those who whispered, laughed, and screamed in this place long ago, as if the wind somehow had captured those voices and continues to hold them in its eddies and currents.

Last spring, on another trip to this area, I did as Randy suggested. On the flank of Laughlin Peak, southwest of Capulin, I sat near an old, derelict homestead in a small grove of cottonwoods on a grassy slope, and I listened quietly to the sound of the air as it moved toward me through the grasses and trees, wrapped around the stone chimney of the old house, swirled in my ears, and then moved on. A gentle wave of wind that warm spring afternoon, one that swept over me and was gone, followed a minute later by another wave, and another—an endless series of surges from the ocean of air that engulfs the plains.

From the state park I drive north and then west along unpaved ranch roads, their gritty surfaces damp and slick from last night's light snow. In addition to the Santa Fe Trail to the south, I now track the course of Corrumpa Creek to the north.

▼ The Adobe Plains ▼

Ernest Seton-Thompson, a popular turn-of-the-century author and founder of the Boy Scouts of America, celebrated this area in "Lobo: The King of Corrumpaw," a chapter in his book *Wild Animals I Have Known*. In rather florid prose "Lobo" tells the story of a giant wolf that decimated cattle and sheep on the ranches along Corrumpa Creek in the early 1890s. Lobo led a pack of five other wolves, including a white female known as Blanca, supposed to be Lobo's mate. Lobo's "deep roar" boomed down the Corrumpa, and he was so hated and feared by the local ranchers that they eventually offered a $1,000 bounty for his pelt.

Seton-Thompson may have been an admirer of wild animals, but he also was a product of his ecologically unenlightened times. A friend of one of the ranchers, he offered to rid the area of this "grizzly devastator," and he set about with dogs, traps, and poison to do so. But Lobo proved more cunning than Seton-Thompson had anticipated. He avoided tainted meat, and he deliberately sprang the traps Seton-Thompson set for him. (Even after realizing its ineffectiveness, Seton-Thompson continued to use poison, but only because "it was meanwhile a sure means of killing many prairie wolves [coyotes] and other destructive vermin.") Finally Seton-Thompson was forced to target the reckless Blanca as a means of getting Lobo.

"She was the handsomest wolf I had ever seen," Seton-Thompson wrote of the trapped white wolf, howling with pain and defiance. But his admiration extended only so far. He and his cowboy helper "each threw a lasso

173

over the neck of the doomed wolf, and strained our horses in opposite directions until the blood burst from her mouth, her eyes glazed, her limbs stiffened and then fell limp. Homeward then we rode, carrying the dead wolf, and exulting over this, the first death-blow we had been able to inflict on the Corrumpaw pack." Lobo, bereft over the loss of Blanca, fell into four of the 130 traps Seton-Thompson again set for him. There he lay, bleeding and helpless, for two days and nights before Seton-Thompson arrived on horseback. Rather than strangle or shoot him (and "spoil his royal hide"), Seton-Thompson tied the dying wolf's jaws and feet, carried him back to the ranch, and staked him in a pasture. In the end, however, Lobo may have got the best of Seton-Thompson, completely ignoring the man who had gone to so much effort to subdue him. "He lay calmly on his breast," Seton-Thompson wrote with something like regret, "and gazed with those steadfast yellow eyes away past me down through the gateway of the cañon, over the open plains—his plains—nor moved a muscle when I touched him."

Today, of course, there are no wild wolves in New Mexico. All were exterminated in the same manner as Lobo. Dogs, traps, and poison. All of the major predators of the plains, with the exception of raptors and the irrepressible coyote, have been eradicated. The plains are quiet. The cattle and sheep may graze in safety.

As I drive toward Grenville and the U.S. highway, I can see, off to the south, the small volcanic cone known as Mount Dora. Mount Dora was named by one of the area's best-known characters and scoundrels, Stephen W. Dorsey, supposedly because it resembled a particular physical attribute of his sister-in-law, Medora Peck. (In regional Spanish it is a *tetilla*.) Clayton, which he helped found, is named for one of his sons. The sprawling, idiosyncratic house he built in the foothills south of Laughlin Peak, near Mountain Spring and Point of Rocks on the Santa Fe Trail, is still known as the Dorsey Mansion. Although he lived in New Mexico for only fifteen years, Stephen Dorsey left his imprint on the map of this country.

Born in Vermont, Dorsey attended Oberlin College in Ohio and served in the Union Army during the Civil War, rising to the rank of captain. After the war he amassed a fortune by selling high-risk railroad bonds to unsuspecting Englishmen. Eventually he got into Republican politics and served one term as a senator from Arkansas—amid charges he had bribed his way into Congress—before buying the huge Uña de Gato land grant in New Mexico in 1877.

Dorsey came to New Mexico, built a large log house, and set himself up as a cattle baron. A visiting reporter, transported by Dorsey's legendary charm and the house's opulent furnishings, described it as "quite the correct sort of country home for a gentleman of elegant but good taste."

Unfortunately, the Uña de Gato grant document was discovered to be a forgery, clouding Dorsey's title to his ranch, and Dorsey was indicted in a national scandal involving frauds perpetrated on the federal government by contractors of the so-called star mail routes. The *New York Times* alleged that "the amount known to have been pocketed by the Stephen W. Dorsey gang in excess of the amount called for by their original bids is not less in round figures than $412,000." After two long, public trials filled with theatrical flourishes—Dorsey attempted to delay the second trial, for example, by producing affidavits from doctors attesting that he was suffering from amblyopia, nervous prostration, and Bright's disease of the kidneys—Dorsey was acquitted of all charges.

Dorsey, ever the poseur, told reporters, "I have nothing to do now but to go back to my ranch and work as a simple ranchman."

When asked if he was retired from politics, he responded, "Every prudent man ought to be, and certainly a cattleman should not be engaged in that business. My cattle do not vote. I with my wife do our own cooking, and we live in a log house, a building into which no politics can ever enter."

The log house, however, had been significantly embellished by the addition, on its east side, of a large Gothic-revival sandstone structure. The new addition was centered on a crenelated stone tower into which the faces of Dorsey, his wife, Helen, and his brother, John, were carved, and the mansion's landscaped grounds now included a large swimming pool (the water surrounding three islands, one sporting a gazebo), an ornately carved stone fountain, a carriage house, and a large greenhouse-smokehouse. The Dorsey Mansion was completed in 1886, and its owner—the "simple ranchman"—immedi-

ately began entertaining lavishly at his hacienda. To cele-
brate its completion, 110 guests attended a party that
began with dinner, segued into all-night dancing, and
ended with billiards and breakfast (quail on toast). On
another occasion, when Helen was gone, Dorsey is said
to have imported a line of chorus girls from Kansas City.

Dorsey occupied his baronial estate for another
six years, all the time fighting challenges to his land title
and holding creditors, plaintiffs, and homesteaders at
bay, before he tired of the fray. He left New Mexico in
1892, moving to Denver to speculate in water rights and
mining interests. He died in Los Angeles in 1916,
reportedly having spent his last years in one of the most
elegant homes in the city.

The Dorsey Mansion passed through numerous
private owners, slowly deteriorating, until the 1970s,
when it was bought by the state of New Mexico, which
opened it as a state monument. Even the state, however,
tired of the expense of maintaining the decrepit mansion.
In the 1980s it was sold to a small group of California
investors. They spend only a part of the summer there,
having hired a local Hispanic family to live in the cav-
ernous mansion full-time to caretake it.

When I visited the Dorsey Mansion on a bright
May day, one of the new owners gave me a short tour
through the place. She was a young, blond-haired
woman named Sandy, and that year she had arrived from
California only a couple of days before. She seemed distracted or bewildered—I wasn't sure which—and moved
through the house like a ghost, never touching anything.

177

Sandy keeps llamas in one of the old corrals, and she and her partners hope someday to open the mansion as a bed and breakfast.

I drive northwest on U.S. 64, past Sierra Grande and through the old, ramshackle railroad town of Des Moines. It is hard for me to imagine Randy growing up here. He is one of the most urbane people I know and seems quite content living in Phoenix. Yet when I recently discussed with him one of my trips to this area, I detected in his voice an unmistakable note of nostalgia. Although he never would choose to live here again, he has fond memories of his boyhood and obviously misses some aspect of life in this open, unconfined place.

The plains get to people. Before embarking on one of his trips over the Santa Fe Trail, Gregg spoke of "[a]n unconquerable propensity to return to prairie life." And after retiring from the Santa Fe trade, he wrote:

> Since that time [on the Santa Fe Trail] I have striven in vain to reconcile myself to the even tenor of civilized life in the United States; and have sought in its amusements and its society a substitute for those high excitements which have attached me so strongly to Prairie life. Yet I am almost ashamed to confess that scarcely a day passes without my experiencing a pang of regret that I am not now roving at large upon those western plains. Nor do I find my taste peculiar; for I have hardly known a man, who has ever become familiar with the kind of life which I have led for so many years, that has not relinquished it with regret.

▼ The Adobe Plains ▼

In his measured prose Gregg got it exactly right. There is indeed something about this country that strikes deep within us, summons up feelings over which we have little control. Maybe it takes us back to the ancient savanna and the thrill of the hunt, when our very lives depended on the sweep of such open spaces.

At Des Moines I turn onto New Mexico 22 and drive toward Folsom, passing en route Twin Butte Curve, the site of Black Jack Ketchum's last, ill-fated robbery. Today Twin Butte's cinders are being quarried, and one of its mounds has been obliterated.

Just outside of Folsom a sleek, bushy-tailed coyote lopes across the highway in front of me. When I reach the point where it crossed, I slow the car and honk the horn, and the coyote stops and looks back at me, its ears erect, its expression quizzical.

Don't be so damned curious, I find myself thinking. Just keep running.

After a brief tour through the Folsom Museum— the town's attic, filled with items loaned or donated by nearly everyone who lives in Folsom—I drive north toward Branson, Colorado. For a few miles the highway follows the Dry Cimarron River, so named because its healthy flow disappears underground for long stretches before resurfacing downstream. At the intersection with the road up Toll Gate Canyon I check my watch and ponder the wisdom of continuing this detour. Despite the late hour, however, something urges me up the canyon, across the high grasslands on Black Mesa, and into Colorado. I am not disappointed.

From the outskirts of Branson the view is breathtaking. To the west the Spanish Peaks loom up in startling relief; behind them the snowy ridge of Culebra snakes across the horizon. Toward the north the Crestones and Kit Carson rise craggily behind the Front Range, and beyond the valley of the Arkansas River the summit of Pikes Peak floats wraithlike against a white winter sky. Farther around the compass the plains stretch toward Nebraska and Kansas, and, farther still, Black Mesa reaches into the Oklahoma panhandle. Huge grassy coves, each comprising thousands of acres, indent the northern edge of the mesa. The land feels infinite.

This is the West, I am thinking. This is what we came here for.

In failing light I circle the crater at Capulin volcano. The wind has calmed, and the temperature has dropped to near zero. Six or eight inches of snow cover the trail, and the north sides of the piñon and juniper trees are blasted with ice. A snow squall envelops Laughlin Peak and obscures the view in that direction, but to the east I can see Rabbit Ear Mountain and Black Mesa, subtle landmarks on the gently curving earth. The twilight is very still.

This land has always attracted people who perceived in its spaciousness different kinds of opportunity. The great Indian tribes of the plains, the nameless Mexican buffalo hunters, Josiah Gregg and the Santa Fe traders, Goodnight and Loving, Stephen W. Dorsey, Black Jack Ketchum. And so it attracted its first settlers over a century ago. They made their homes here and set about to tame its wildness. For a time it seemed they had succeeded. The Indians were subdued, the outlaws brought to frontier justice, the wild animals exterminated. The railroad came through, and towns grew along it. But the land itself remained implacable. Years passed, and wells went dry, grasses withered, and the wind blew without relief. The people stood their ground against the onslaught of the elements, huddled together, survived; but at their feet the ancient dream of a cattleman's empire lay dormant on the cracked earth, like a dry seed in a dry season.

Gallup

West from Albuquerque on I-40, following old Route 66. Beyond Stuckey's and the dilapidated gas station at Rio Puerco. The March wind whipping under gray clouds. Past Mesita and Old Laguna. Into Indian country. ("Tax Free Cigarettes," the Casa Blanca Store advertises.) By Acomita and McCartys. Racing a westbound Santa Fe freight between red sandstone mesas and across black lava flows. Around Mount Taylor (Tsah Dzil, one of the Navajos' four sacred mountains) and deeper into Indian country.

West from Grants, between the Wingate cliffs and the snowy Zuni Mountains. Past the first hogan, the earth around it sheep-trodden and gray. Across the high grasslands, over the continental divide, and past a fading yellow Whiting Brothers Motel. (Oh, Route 66.) By the Giant Truck Stop, down the Rio Puerco of the west, and along a string of loud billboards: "Gilbert Ortega's—

50%–60% off Indian Jewelry!" "Tobe Turpen Trading Company—On the Zuni Highway!"

Finally the cut through the hogback and the town itself strung along the railroad tracks, gaudy colors and neon lights in the dusk, streets crowded with pickup trucks and cars, small groups of Indians straggling down the sidewalks and standing on the corners huddled against the wind.

Gallup. The mere mention of its name to anyone in New Mexico commonly elicits a response of disgust or dismay, because Gallup is known, more than anything else, for its highly visible alcohol problems. Specifically, its Native American alcohol problems. Bluntly, the drunk Indians on its streets.

"Can Gallup Solve Its Alcohol Ills?" a headline in the May 8, 1988, *Albuquerque Journal* asked, and the newspaper devoted an entire section to trying to answer that question. Three years later Conroy Chino, an investigative reporter for television station KOAT in Albuquerque, did a week-long exposé on Gallup's alcohol problem, as if he were uncovering it for the first time.

The problem, however, is not new. Gallup has always been a reservation border town (or, more accurately, a town located near the borders of several Indian reservations where liquor sales are illegal), and as long as it has existed, Indians have gone there to drink. Only the numbers change. In 1987, to take a recent example, Gallup city police arrested 885 people for DWI, and the protective custody van picked up more than twenty-eight thousand people and transported them to the drunk tank to sober up overnight. Two years later residents marched from Gallup to Santa Fe to lobby for tougher liquor sales legislation, and the former mayor, Ed Muñoz, made national headlines by publicizing the problem and trying to curb liquor sales. But the problem does not go away.

Everyone who has visited or lived in Gallup has stories. I have mine. In the summer of 1985, when I worked in Chaco Canyon, I saw the Albuquerque television news only twice. Both times, a Navajo had been killed by a train in Gallup. One had passed out on the tracks, and the other had walked uncomprehendingly into the whistling locomotive. And another: In the summer of 1987, when I worked and lived in Gallup, I accompanied one of my bosses to a picnic at McGaffey, in the Zuni Mountains east of town. As we were driving home on the interstate at twilight, we had to swerve toward the median to avoid a glazed-eyed Navajo teen-ager, staggering toward us in the right-hand lane of traffic.

If you were an Indian, Leslie Marmon Silko wrote in *Ceremony*, you didn't linger in Gallup. "[Y]ou attended to business and then left, and you were never in that town after dark. That was the warning the old Zunis, and Hopis, and Navajos had about Gallup. The safest way was to avoid the bad places after dark." That is Gallup's image, drawn from the reality of its streets. But it is not the only truth about the town, and perhaps not even the most interesting.

Its past is a chapter out of our history. In 1880, twelve years after the Navajo reservation had been established along what is now the Arizona–New Mexico state line, a saloon and general store called the Blue Goose opened between Fort Wingate and Fort Defiance. The next year surveyors laid the route of the Atlantic and Pacific Railway, the predecessor of the Santa Fe, through the area. Coal was discovered in the nearby hills, and Gallup became a major rail stop. It was named either for a locomotive engineer or a local paymaster for the railroad.

Chinese helped construct the railroad, and Italians and Slavs were brought in to mine the coal. Anglo businessmen opened stores, bars, and banks, and Hispanic shepherds grazed their flocks on the grasslands to the east, near Grants and Bluewater. Navajos, Hopis, Zunis, Acomas, and Lagunas came to trade.

"Gallup became a frontier town in the noisiest tradition," Frank Waters wrote in *Masked Gods*,

> with cowpokes riding in every Saturday night to shoot up its row of saloons and gambling halls. . . .
>
> From the Navaho reservation came the traders in wagons piled high with wool and pulled by ten spans of horses. Other traders moved in from remote trading posts to establish large trading companies. Gallup became the trading and shipping center of the whole area.
>
> Always there came Indians—a continuous straggle of Zunis on foot and Navahos on spooky, quick-stepping ponies, to gawk and trade.
>
> This was Gallup. The trading capital. The Indian capital. The metropolis of the Four Corners.
>
> And this is Gallup today. Saloons and trading posts, bars and stores catering to the Indian trade. The Blue Goose infinitely and repetitiously multiplied.

Waters wrote that in 1950, but it could have been written last year. Gallup does not change. It is impervious to change: 1900, 1950, 1990—all the same. It is the last authentic frontier town. It is, as its chamber of commerce proclaims, the heart of the Indian country. It is the edge of the modern world, the place where, even today, even here, in our modern republic, people struggle daily against poverty, disease, and early death—the ancient enemies of the race.

This gray March day I leave the interstate at exit twenty-two, Montoya Boulevard / Miyamura Drive / Miyamura Park. During the years I worked in Chaco, I sometimes shopped in Gallup. During those visits I acquired the habit of filling up my car at Miyamura's Exxon on old Route 66 on the west side of town. Hershey Miyamura, the proprietor, was a gentle, middle-aged man of Japanese ancestry who always had time to chat for a few minutes and who first directed me to Genaro's Restaurant, home of the hottest green chile in New Mexico. It was several years later, after Hershey Miyamura retired and his gas station closed, that I learned that Miyamura Drive and Park were named after him, a Gallup native and Congressional Medal of Honor winner.

After checking into the El Rancho Hotel, I call my friend John to confirm our dinner plans, then wander down to inspect the lobby. Originally opened in 1937 and restored and reopened in 1988, the El Rancho is an architectural oddity—a sprawling stone and wood ranch-style building with unexpected antebellum flourishes (white columns out front, for example). A perfectly decent place to stay, it aspires to be an elegant south-western hotel. The dimly lit lobby is filled with dark, varnished wood and display cases of Indian jewelry, and its walls are decorated with deer trophies and Navajo rugs. Above the front desk a heavy wooden frame encloses four sand-painting clocks, each depicting, in dramatic silhouette, an Indian brave on horseback, each assigned to a different time zone.

Around the upper level of the two-story lobby are photographs of the various Hollywood stars who stayed at the El Rancho in its heyday, during the 1930s and 1940s, when numerous westerns were filmed in the Gallup area. John Wayne, Alan Ladd, Randolph Scott. Most are typical Hollywood press-release portraits, but the one of Tom Mix—showing our hero surrounded by five or six actors costumed as Indians, the whole bunch shot through a shattered spider web in high-contrast black and white—appears surreal, almost psychedelic.

An hour later, over dinner at Pedro's Mexican restaurant, John and I chat about his adopted hometown. An archeologist by training, John now works in historic preservation for the Navajo Tribe. He and his wife, Alexa, also an archeologist, have lived in Gallup for four years, but John has spent most of his professional life in and around the area.

He is lanky and cowboyish, and dressed tonight, as usual, in a snap-button shirt, jeans, and dirty boots. He was born and raised in rural New Mexico and speaks with a vestigial ranch drawl, but he is anything but unsophisticated. Possessed of keen native intelligence, he is an acute observer of the world around him. I ask him if he likes living here.

"I do," he says in a tone that indicates he knows the listener expects the opposite answer. "It's funny—for all its reputation as a town where bad things happen to people, Gallup is not a violent town. At least it's not a town where intentional violence is very common. It's just your average small town, with a bunch of people living on the streets on the weekends."

He pauses. Although his demeanor is often laconic (in the best cowboy tradition), John is, on certain subjects, an inveterate storyteller. Life in Indian country is one of those subjects. Right now he is gathering himself.

"Like a lot of people in small towns," he continues after a minute, "a friend of mine never locks his door. Well, he came home one day and realized that someone had been inside his house. He searched all the rooms and didn't find anything missing or anyone there. Then he looked in the refrigerator and discovered that someone had come into his house, walked past his stereo, his television—all the usual stuff that burglars take—and stolen a can of beer. That's all. A can of beer. That's Gallup.

"You see things here you don't see—couldn't see—anywhere else. Last year I was at the Shalimar, one of the dance clubs in town. And this sort of geriatric hippie band from California was playing folk and bluegrass music. When the fiddler began playing 'Orange Blossom Special,' this Navajo guy got up and started clogging.

He was in his early forties and had long hair in braids and was wearing hobnailed boots—he could have been a Vietnam vet. Anyway, the fiddler kept playing faster and faster, and this guy kept dancing faster and faster, and soon everybody was watching and clapping. And finally the fiddler broke it off and said, 'Man, you're good.' And the Navajo made a little bow and accepted the applause. It was . . . well, sort of a transcendent moment.

"And the next day people may see him and think he's just another drunk on the street."

He pauses to fiddle with his food for a minute, then continues.

"A friend of mine who works for the Santa Fe Railroad told me that the engineers play the tom-tom song with the whistle when they see Indians along the tracks, and the Indians love it. They shout and give war whoops as the train passes. It's like they're all reliving the past, or at least some skewed Hollywood version of it.

"By the way, last year the Santa Fe changed its locomotive colors back to red and yellow, and you know what they call that combination? 'Warbonnet.'"

He shakes his head and allows himself a little smile. When he speaks again, his voice is hushed and excited.

"When the new Wal-Mart at the mall opened here, it was a big deal. And you know what? They invited a Navajo medicine man to consecrate it. To bless the Wal-Mart. I love it. By the way, the Gallup store is supposed to be one of the highest grossing in the country. Those Navajos love their Wal-Mart.

"It's life on the edge here. A real multicultural, multiethnic pig show. I guess that's why I like it."

Knowing that I live in Santa Fe now, he looks at me and narrows his eyes, smiling. "I like Gallup," he says finally, "because it's not Santa Fe."

After returning to the hotel, I spend a few minutes perusing the Gallup telephone book.

It is filled with the Hispanic surnames common in New Mexico: Garcia, Gonzales, Lopez, Martinez, Ortega, Ortiz, Padilla, Trujillo. And the Navajo: Begay, Benally, Bitsie, Joe, Nez, Shorty, Tso, Tsosie, Yazzie.

The Italians are easy to spot: Balducci, Bonaguidi, Caviggia, DePauli, DiPomazio (Angelo and Nick, among many others), Peretti, Rocco, Guido Zecca. (I recall that one of my bosses here had a client in town—an elderly woman, a lifelong resident—who spoke only Italian.)

I find the Slavs: Mahalovich, Marusich, Petranovich, Petrovich, Radosevich, Starkovich, Tomljamovich, Yurkovich. And a few Poles: Matlosz, Tomczak. And others I can't identify precisely, though surely of Eastern European origin: Hren, Hoeksema, Plese, Milan Sklenar.

Without doubt Gallup is the most ethnically diverse town in New Mexico. The chamber of commerce reports that its population is 35 percent Hispanic, 20 percent Indian, and 40 percent "Anglo." It is a racial salad—lightly tossed, heavily seasoned.

I wake the next morning to four or five inches of fresh wet snow. The sky is sodden, and the wind is whipping out of the west. Gallup has the cruelest weather of any place in New Mexico. This past winter it was, for a couple of days, the coldest spot in the United States, reaching –33°F one night in late December. Such extremes are not uncommon.

John's theory, explained to me over dinner, is that the prevailing westerly winds funnel through Lupton Gap in Arizona and howl through Gallup and that winter storms back up against the continental divide—a sort of meteorological venturi.

"Upon it impartially, too, descends the weather," Frank Waters wrote. "Gallup has more kinds of weather per hour and square foot than any place you can find. You can be stuck there by snow in May, by rain in October, by driving sand in March. The heat is scorching. The cold is freezing. And the wind keeps blowing through the cracks of all seasons."

This wild March morning I drive west on old Route 66, past the strip of pawn shops and bars facing the railroad tracks. The Navajo Trading Company, Billy K's Pawn, Richardson's Trading Company and Cash Pawn. The Liberty Bar and the Commercial Club. Like stores around Times Square, most have iron bars over their doors and windows—protection from the people on the street. The Lexington Hotel, a grimy, disintegrating brick building, advertises "Public Showers." The road itself is constructed of concrete segments, potholed and cracked, worn, it seems, from the weather and traffic of a hundred years. Dirty slush splashes onto the sidewalks.

As I usually do when I am in this area, I tune the radio to AM 660, KTNN, the voice of the Navajo Nation.

Although we have heard little about it in Santa Fe, there has been a serious measles epidemic on the reservation, and this morning the deejay announces that people who visited the Fort Defiance Indian Health Service Hospital on Wednesday or Friday of this past week may have been accidentally exposed to the virus. Same old sad story.

I turn and circle onto U.S. 666 (the two-laned highway from Gallup to Shiprock, numbered, perhaps, by some crazed, apocalyptic engineer), cross the railroad tracks, and turn into one of the new stations near the interstate to buy gas. The bills I receive in change from the cashier, though of recent issue, are tattered, limp, and oily, as all paper money in Gallup seems to be. These bills have already been counted over hundreds of cash registers, passed through hundreds of roughened hands, been stuffed in hundreds of sweaty pockets. This is an eddy in the current of commerce—a place where money, like time, seems to circle slowly around a shady, green pool.

Later in the morning I sit with John in the small but airy dining room of his modest house on the near south side of town. We have a view of Ford Park directly below, of the railroad tracks and the interstate, of the neighborhoods on the hilly north side of Gallup, and, beyond, of the mesas and canyons of Indian country. Alexa is working in her study, and occasionally we hear her talking on the phone, opening file drawers, rummaging around. Their five dogs, all strays picked up on the reservation, are sitting on the back porch, ears alert, noses planted to the sliding glass door.

"At Halloween," John is saying, "it seems like all the trucks from the reservation come and park down on old Route 66, and they let out their kids, and this procession comes up the hill to the rich neighborhood, hitting us on the way. Last Halloween I counted over two hundred trick or treaters. I had to go to the store to buy more candy."

He smiles. "Those Navajos know how to work the system."

When I knew him at Chaco many years ago, John was as restless as I, as restless as the freight train lurching and clanking through town below us. Now he seems at home here, in this improbable place. What don't you like about Gallup, I ask.

He pauses for a minute, looking out the window, apparently pondering the question.

"It's ugly and dirty," he says finally. "Visually, I mean. Just look at it. The houses are ticky-tacky—there's no distinctive architecture here—and painted shit-brown. The north side looks like little Juarez with those shanties stacked up the hill. And when it's wet, like today," he continues, beginning to relish the description, "the coal seams in the hills ooze black, and the streets and parking lots are sticky with sludge from the pickups that come in from the reservation. It's just ugly."

I ask about the different groups of people in town, and John chooses to enumerate by profession: "The Indian Health Service, which is mostly white; the BIA, which today is mostly Indian; the railroad people, at least what's left of them; the local businessmen and

Indian traders; and of course the reservation Indians, who come into town on the weekends. People tend to socialize within their group, although everyone seems tolerant of everyone else. Gallup is not a racist town, at least not like a lot of towns where you have different ethnic groups living in proximity.

"Indians don't run Gallup—far from it—but, given a choice, it's the town where they prefer to shop and socialize. In order of preference, it's Gallup, Phoenix, and Albuquerque. Farmington only if they're desperate. They feel at home here.

"I know Gallup has a bad reputation. When I was a kid and we were passing through here on vacation, my mother always told us to lock our car doors. Gallup was the place where a drunk Indian might come up to the car at a stoplight and ask for a handout. But I think the number of people who live on the streets—the number of chronic drinkers, true alcoholics—is relatively small. Sure, lots of Indians occasionally go on binges—they're no different than anyone else. It's just that they tend to come to Gallup to do it.

"When I worked for the BIA here, my boss, who was an Indian, had to send some of the crew home one morning because they showed up drunk. After he did it, he said to me, 'I've always wondered who all those drunk Indians are, and it's us!' Sort of a variation on the old 'Pogo' line. And at the tribal offices in Window Rock everybody cuts out photographs of protective custody from the *Independent*, adds funny captions, and tapes them to their office doors. Like archeologists cutting out and taping up 'Far Side' cartoons. They know how to laugh. What happens to some people here may be sad, tragic even, but at least they can find some humor in it. They know how to do that.

"You wanna hear something funny?" he asks, and I can tell from his tone and arched eyebrows that he's about to offer an ironic observation on someone or something close to both of us. "I know most of the archeologists in town, and I never see them anywhere—not in restaurants, not in stores. They don't shop on Saturdays when the rest of us do. It's like they're trying to avoid everybody. I don't know what they do or where they do it."

He shakes his head. "One component of Gallup's population you never see on the street; one component you always see."

He pauses for a minute, recouping his train of thought. "Alexa and I tend to socialize with a couple of the old-time Indian traders here. Our friend Lynn grew up in the trading business and spends more time with Indians than with white people, and—it's hard to describe—he's adopted Indian mannerisms. The inflection of his speech, his body language. He feels more comfortable around Indians than around most white people. I once asked his wife, Cathy, when they were going to move to Phoenix to make their fortune. 'Never,' she snapped back. 'How do you expect my husband to survive without a hundred and forty thousand Navajos in his lap every day?'"

Alexa wanders into the dining room. She has overheard bits of our conversation.

"It's really very funny and odd," she says. "I belong to this group called the American Association of University Women. They're all white and college educated. Having a college degree is the requirement for joining—that pretty much eliminates all of the Hispanic and Indian women in town. What's more, none of these women are from Gallup. And they sit around and talk about ways they can improve Gallup, and after a while you realize that what they want to do is change Gallup into wherever it is they came from. I think Gallup scares them. But speaking as an anthropologist, what scares them interests me.

"When John and I first moved to town, we were given a temporary guest membership to the Gallup Country Club, up on the hill. We went to a few functions there. It's typical Gallup—this private club that tries to be very fancy, with a golf course and everything, and just across the highway is a little rural tenement. Just a bunch of dilapidated trailers with no electricity and little corn plots out back. And every time we went to the club, something was wrong with the place. Either the plumbing had backed up, or the swimming pool had cracked, or the electrical circuits had blown. It got to be very funny—this fancy country club where nothing ever worked."

After John and I eat lunch at Genaro's—a Mexican restaurant with an Italian name and a Navajo and Hispanic clientele located in the west-side neighborhood known locally as Chihuahuita—I drive over to visit my former boss, Jay.

Jay is a successful small-town lawyer, a devout Catholic, and the happily beleaguered father of five kids. He is an unassuming man, hiding the fact that he is known and respected professionally throughout the state and was in college a world-class distance runner. He and his wife, Kitty, live in a sprawling brick house near the Gallup Indian Medical Center. When I arrive this cool afternoon, Jay is watching the University of Kansas, his alma mater, in the NCAA basketball tournament. Kitty is doing mountains of laundry. The kids are running amok. It is a stereotypical suburban scene.

I talked to Jay on the telephone before coming here for this visit. Knowing he likes living in Gallup, I asked him why, and he responded in a manner that now reminds me of John's answer to that same question.

"Oh, I don't know," he said. "Because of the small-town atmosphere and the cultural diversity, I suppose. It's a good place to raise kids. It's safe, but it's not sheltered from the problems of the world. It's a good place to do work that makes a difference. So many people here make a contribution. Unlike, say, Santa Fe," he observed wryly, "where so many people contribute so little."

Jay asks if I have plans for that evening, and when I say no, he and Kitty insist that I accompany them to the annual Saint Patrick's Day party at the home of some of their church friends.

"Unless you'll feel threatened," Jay says, his voice filled with mischief, "by a bunch of crazed papists."

The party is a gala affair. The price of admission this year is the requirement that everyone (except out-of-town guests) perform something Irish—sing an Irish ballad, recite a W. B. Yeats poem, act in a bawdy skit. The priest and the bishop are there, and during a break in the action I strike up a conversation with an attractive middle-aged woman named June. June is from San Diego and makes her living doing computer research for the University of California. But she is moved to do charitable work, and she is living temporarily in Gallup, where she teaches English to Mexican postulants at the Missionaries of Charity, an order of nuns that operates a soup kitchen on the north side of town. June exudes an inner calm, and her eyes shine with excitement when she talks about her dream of eventually going to Calcutta to assist Mother Theresa in her work.

Later in the evening I talk to one of Jay's law partners, David, and his wife, Natalie. They are preparing to leave Gallup to return to Indiana, near where David went to law school, in order to be closer to medical care for a son with spinal bifida. Natalie is intelligent and intense, and although young, she takes the world's problems to heart. The family lives in an older house in town that was formerly a soup kitchen, and she tells me she can't help but feed the vagrants and street people who occasionally still come to the door. Natalie doesn't want to leave New Mexico but knows it is best for the family. So she and David are going.

Toward the end of the evening the men congregate around the pool table at one end of the living room, and the host passes out Churchill-sized cigars to all who want them. There are off-color jokes, and small bets are placed on the outcome of eight ball. The wives accept this caricature of manly behavior with good-natured tolerance, sitting together at the other end of the room, occasionally shaking their heads at their husbands, talking and laughing quietly among themselves.

The next morning breaks clear, calm, and warm. Winter one day, spring the next. I check out of the hotel and drive slowly west along Coal Avenue. Near downtown I stop to photograph one of Gallup's steep side streets and a massive stone retaining wall behind which a house has been constructed on fill dirt. As I stand on the sidewalk, a young Navajo man comes out of the building behind me and asks what I'm doing.

Just taking pictures of the houses, I say.

"Why?" he asks.

I tell him that I lived here once and that I'm interested in the way people in Gallup built their houses up the sides of the hills.

"I work at the radio station," he says, nodding his head toward the building, which I now see features a marquee with radio call letters on it. "I'm the morning deejay. I just put on a six-minute song, so I thought I would take a break and come outside."

What song? I ask.

"'Hotel California,' by the Eagles," he says carefully, watching me out of the corners of his eyes to catch my reaction.

He speaks quietly and with a slight staccato, as most Navajos do when speaking English. He is a handsome young man, stout but not fat, with a friendly, inquisitive face.

"I'm Eddie Yazzie," he says, offering his hand and shaking mine softly.

Eddie lives about thirty-five miles west of Gallup, near Lupton, Arizona, and hitchhikes or drives his family's car to work every day. I ask him if he ever broadcasts in Navajo.

"No. I understand Navajo, but I don't speak it very well. I got this job," he says with what seems to be a mixture of sheepishness and pride, "because my English is pretty good."

We stand for a few minutes in the warm sunlight on the Sunday-morning sidewalk, conversing quietly, listening to the chatter of the early-spring birds in the still-leafless trees. It is a peaceful interlude.

"I'll be seein' you," he says finally as he turns to go back inside. I ask him where he is on the dial.

"FM 90.3. K-Q-ninety-three." He smiles, and his voice deepens and resonates. "Tune me in."

I cut up to Green Street and down toward the post office. I stop to photograph 204 East Green, the duplex where I lived during the summer I worked in Gallup. The house was built in the 1920s of cream-colored brick and at that time would have been a substantial dwelling in a good part of town; but by my time here it had entered a state of neglect and decay, its high ceilings flaky and discolored with age, its hardwood floors bare and scratched. The house was furnished with a few odd pieces—an old vinyl-covered armchair and footstool, a laminated coffee table—and I spent the summer sleeping on a twin bed in the living room, eating my meals on a borrowed card table, and listening to cassettes on my boom box. The days were often warm, but at night a cool westerly breeze always wafted in through the high, open windows. That breeze also carried the twilight sounds of the neighborhood: cars cruising slowly down the street, kids playing on the sidewalk, and, from other houses, the indistinct murmur of television shows, radio music, and voices speaking in English, Spanish, and Navajo. Occasionally Jay stopped by after dinner—either alone or with the family—and took me off to dessert or one of his civic meetings.

It seems much longer ago than four years. At that time I was mourning the loss of a woman I had loved quite madly, and I often sat up late at the card table filling my journal with the soulful longings of the broken-hearted. It was a peculiarly solitary summer, one of the last of my youth, and I remember it now with unabashed fondness and a twinge of nostalgia.

I turn up First Street, climb the steep hill, and park my car around the curve. I then walk back to photograph John's favorite house in town, a white matchbox with green trim, hanging on the side of the hill.

As I am returning to the car, one of the neighbors approaches me—he and his teen-aged son have been working on a car in his driveway—and asks me politely what I'm doing. When I tell him I'm photographing houses in Gallup, he brightens and tells me that he and his wife do the same thing when they're traveling. His curiosity satisfied—or his suspicions assuaged—we engage in easy conversation as we stand in the street.

His name is Gil Rojas, and he is a teacher at the high school. Born in Gallup, he grew up on the north side, in an area he points out to me from where we stand, far across the railroad tracks, the interstate, and the Rio Puerco. He owns the matchbox house as well as two others on the block, and he points out a dogleg in First Street below us, created when the people who built the houses in this block misjudged the extension of the street up the hill.

"Nothin' in Gallup, even a straight line, ever comes out quite right," he says with a laugh.

"Except the interstate, I guess," he continues. "It was supposed to bypass the town to the south, but the local business people were worried that Gallup would die without the traffic, so they raised a fuss, and the highway department eventually put it right straight through the middle of town.

"I don't like that thing. Look at it. It's ugly—a big wall through the middle of Gallup. Cuts the town in half. Separates us from each other. And it causes a hell of a flooding problem. Any engineer could have looked at the drainage pattern off these hills and seen that all the water flows into the Rio Puerco. But the highway department didn't. They just built the thing like a big dam. So now all the water flows down and floods the streets where they pass under the interstate."

He laughs again, shaking his head. I sense that he really doesn't like the interstate, but his laugh is not malicious or condescending. He simply is laughing at our common human foibles. Although I've known him for only ten minutes, already I like Gil Rojas.

For no particular reason I tell him that I find Gallup the most interesting and ethnically diverse town in New Mexico.

"Yeah, ol' Gallup," he says fondly. "There's no other town like it. It's a real melting pot. But you know, everybody gets along here. In Gallup you can call an Indian an Indian, an Italian an Italian, and a Mexican a Mexican, and nobody gets mad. The new mayor, Galanis, is a Greek, but he's a Gallup Greek. His family's been here a long time.

"We used to have a lot of Chinese and Japanese, too. They came in with the railroad, but most of them are gone now. Do you see that big house on the hill," he says, pointing to a stucco monstrosity far away on the north side. "The old Chinese cemetery is just below it. When I was a kid, I used to play around it, but I don't know how much is left now. A lot of the headstones were vandalized or stolen.

"Back in the old days we were prejudiced. Even in Gallup. We didn't let the Chinese bury their dead with the Christians."

He is quiet for a minute, staring off toward the old cemetery. He seems saddened by the memory.

Finally he looks at his son, who has been standing with us patiently while we talk.

"Well, we should get back to work and let you get on your way. Good luck to you, my friend."

We shake hands and I walk up the hill, feeling good about the day, feeling good about the place.

I meander through town, find my way to 666, cross the railroad tracks, and turn onto the entrance ramp to the interstate, heading east. The sky is bright, and the mesas all around are vivid with color.

Gallup—the town that doesn't hide its ugliness and its wounded, bleeding humanity. Or, for that matter, the chambers of its heart. It is the world in microcosm, in all its variety and texture, filled with pain and love. In his flamboyant style Frank Waters may have captured the character of the town best when he wrote, "Yet we all— all we Wops and Dagoes, Greasers, Gringos and Indians—seem bound together here as nowhere else by some strange enchantment that dismisses all this misery, poverty, and shabby sinfulness as a transient chronicle of human error. . . ."

As I drive east, I tune in 90.3 on the FM dial. "Mercy, Mercy Me," by Marvin Gaye, is playing, and for some reason that song, with its soulful lyrics, its sweet voice, and its haunting melody, seems oddly appropriate. The deejay doesn't come on before I pass out of the station's range near the continental divide, but I imagine Eddie Yazzie sitting in his dark cubicle, watching the record spin, reading a magazine, getting ready to send his patter to the reservation and the world.

The Boot Heel

West of Las Cruces the interstate leaves the Mesilla Valley and strikes across the Chihuahuan desert. Ahead, vast flats of creosote and mesquite stretch toward hazy peaks that shimmer and float on the horizon like ghost ships on an arid ocean. For an hour the prospect hardly changes. Then, just east of Deming, the Florida Mountains rise in a dark, jagged mass beside the highway. Mineral-rich and heavily prospected, the Floridas and the other small ranges in the area—Cooke's Peak to the north and the Tres Hermanas to the south—supply a thriving cottage industry in ores and semiprecious stones. "Elvis Buys Rocks!" and "Topless Geodes!" homemade billboards along the shoulder tease.

I leave the interstate at Deming and head south on New Mexico 81. This part of the state, renowned for its pure underground waters (the subsurface flow of the Mimbres River) and its mild climate, has become, in recent years, a favorite winter roost for cash-poor snow-birds. A sign along the highway indicates the headquar-ters of the Luna County Ranchette Owners Association, and a few miles south of town an elaborate, lovingly maintained rock-and-cactus garden surrounds a tidy pre-fab home. (In front of the house a plastic ostrich sticks its neck in the ground, its head reappearing a few feet away.)

Farther south I pass fields of white-flecked cotton and acres of green-leafed chiles laden, this warm October afternoon, with pendulous red fruit. A sign on the east side of the highway advertises a pistachio orchard for sale "with water rights." Finally, on the outskirts of Colum-bus, a grizzled man wearing a stained cowboy hat, greasy sheepskin jacket, faded jeans, and dirty cowboy boots pedals an ancient bicycle toward the border.

Her hair is as white as cotton and cut short around her head. Although she appears frail sitting behind the counter, a metal cane at her side, her eyes are alert and her manner is direct. As I step through the screen door of the Columbus Historical Museum, she addresses me in a firm, well-practiced voice.

"Welcome to our museum. Please sign the guest register. Where are you from?"

When I answer Santa Fe, she pauses and narrows her eyes. Something I have said has caught her attention, distracted her from her routine.

"Oh," she says deliberately. "Well." Then: "I feel I should tell you that we don't think much of your politicians up there."

I laugh, taken aback momentarily by her forth-rightness, which seems to be exactly that: forthright-ness, not malice. I ask her why she thinks badly of our politicians.

"We think they tend to ignore us down here in the southern part of the state. We think they spend all of our money in Santa Fe."

I nod and smile and tell her that wouldn't sur-prise me at all.

"We've been trying to get the road between here and El Paso paved for twenty years. Well. Come in any-way. Welcome."

Her name is Faun Homman, and she is the vol-unteer docent at the museum. In her evenly paced, pleas-ant voice she orients me to Columbus. The museum building, she explains, is the old Columbus railroad depot. Built in 1902 by Phelps Dodge Corporation, the line, known as the border railroad, transported surplus copper ore from Douglas, Arizona, to smelters in El Paso. Phelps Dodge eventually sold the line to Southern Pacific, which operated passenger trains along it until 1961. Then SP abandoned the line, tore up the tracks, and donated the right-of-way to the state. The unpaved road to El Paso follows the old right-of-way.

"Sixty-five miles to El Paso on that road. One hundred and thirty via Deming and Las Cruces. But we don't recommend that tourists go that way. There are loose rocks on the roadbed, and a lot of people have had flat tires along it recently."

I ask her if she's lived in Columbus her entire life.

"Oh no. I taught school in Minneapolis for forty-six years, then retired here eighteen years ago."

Do you like it?

"Oh yes. The climate is wonderful. Could you ask for a nicer day than today?"

I shake my head no. Do you miss the city? I ask.

"No, not much. Some of the cultural activities—theater, concerts. But these days Minneapolis, like all big cities, has too much crime. Here nobody locks their doors. Columbus is a nice quiet town."

How many people live here?

"Columbus has 647 people. They say that Palomas, across the border, has 7,000. The Mexicans have a big industrial park. Since the railroad left, Columbus doesn't have much. The port of entry. The state park. That's about it. But if the road to El Paso ever gets paved, Columbus will boom."

As we chat, a group of four elderly snowbirds wanders in. I thank Faun for her time.

"You're very welcome," she says with a slight nod of her head.

As I edge into the depot's old waiting room to begin my museum tour, Faun greets the snowbirds: "Welcome to our museum. Please sign the guest register. Where are you from?"

The museum is cluttered with artifacts local and exotic: prehistoric pots from nearby Nuevo Casas Grandes, a small Olmec-style stone head from southern Mexico, metates from Chaco Canyon. And many photographs and assorted memorabilia from the era when Pancho Villa's forces made history by raiding Columbus. The only attack by a foreign power on American soil, the town now boasts. It came early on the morning of March 9, 1916, during the tumult of the Mexican revolution.

Born Doroteo Arango, the charismatic Villa was also known by his nom de guerre, *El Tigre del Norte*. Utilizing his famed *Dorados* (literally "golden"; Villa's best cavalry), he pursued his dream (of conquest? of true Mexican democracy?) across the Sierra Madre and through the deserts of Chihuahua and Sonora. During the revolution's early years he was the darling of the American media and attracted numerous American supporters, including Ambrose Bierce and, by some accounts, the future western-movie star Tom Mix (who allegedly rode for a short time with Villa's *Dorados*). Eventually, however, Villa fell into disfavor with Woodrow Wilson's administration, which recognized Venustiano Carranza's Constitutionalist regime. After the United States allowed Carranza's troops to ride the border railroad to inflict a devastating defeat on Villa at Agua Prieta, Sonora, in 1915, Villa developed a pathological hatred of this country. Many historians think that his ill-advised attack on Columbus (he lost more than one hundred troops compared to eighteen American fatalities, most of them civilians) was motivated as much by personal enmity as by any strategic plan. After the Columbus raid and General John J. Pershing's "punitive expedition" into Mexico, Villa's political influence waned. On July 20, 1923, he and four bodyguards were assassinated in Parral, Chihuahua, by a group of local men whose motives remain obscure.

Today there is not much evidence of Villa's raid in Columbus—the artifacts in the museum (including a plaster death mask of Villa) and, curiously, a small state park named after the man who ransacked and burned most of the town seventy-five years ago.

West of Columbus New Mexico 9 follows the border through a Chihuahuan desert gilded by late-afternoon light. The faint, tarry odor of creosote permeates the air, and tall yuccas sprout out of the cinders on the old railroad bed. Grasshoppers the size of spark plugs teem on the highway. Between Columbus and the derelict town of Hermanas I pass a few fields of chiles, irrigated from an underground bolson, and a few unmarked ranch roads. Otherwise the desert appears undisturbed. Except for a Border Patrol Blazer and a couple of pickups, there is no traffic.

This corner of New Mexico, known as the Boot Heel, nicks the northwest corner of Chihuahua. By my definition at least, the Boot Heel comprises that part of the state that lies south of Deming and west of Columbus, and thus includes lands acquired by the United States not only through the Treaty of Guadalupe Hidalgo in 1848, as was the rest of New Mexico, but also through the Gadsden Purchase in 1853.

Topographically, the Boot Heel consists of parallel, north-south trending mountain ranges (as one travels from east to west, the Big Hatchet, Little Hatchet, Animas, and Peloncillo Mountains) separated by wide basins of Chihuahuan desert. Culturally, it is a land of lonely ranches, disintegrating railroad stops (Columbus, Hachita, Rodeo), a Phelps Dodge company town (Playas), and an old farming crossroads (Animas). And little else. The remote, empty borderland.

I arrive in Hachita as the sun is settling toward the horizon. During the journey that inspired *Blue Highways*, William Least Heat-Moon stopped in Hachita and discovered what he described as "a genuine Western saloon primeval"—the Desert Den Bar & Filling Station. I pull off the highway and cruise slowly down dusty Avenue A, thirsty for a beer and looking for the spot. I don't see the bar, but a cowboy talking to the driver of a pickup on the side of the street tells me that its owner, a woman named Virginia Been, sold her liquor license a few years back, and the bar closed down.

"You cain't buy a beer anywhere in this town anymore," he says with a wry smile and a shake of his head.

Nevertheless, I park the car and walk slowly through the old town, admiring its disintegrating adobes and, at the same time, the well-maintained prefab homes that the children have placed next door. As I walk, I begin to sense the lethargy of a late afternoon in late October in Hachita, New Mexico. Dogs drowse behind fences overgrown with vines, and people converse quietly behind screen doors. A lone rooster crows in the distance. One street over, a car door closes, an engine cranks, and the car drives slowly toward the highway, its tires softly crunching the gravel on the dirt bed. The entire town, although at first sight it appeared deserted, is suffused with a pleasant feeling familiar even in this alien landscape—the comfortable, tired glow at the end of another working day.

As the sun drops behind the Little Hatchet Mountains, I climb into my car, take my leave, and drive slowly south toward Antelope Wells.

A bar of vivid red light—the color of arterial blood—lies across the eastern horizon, grading to magenta higher in the sky and indigo overhead. The stars in the darkened west are myriad, uncountable; the morning air is crystalline.

After a fitful night I have risen early to watch the dawn develop over the Boot Heel. I camped last night on a sandy flat north of the Big Hatchet Mountains, with a view west through Hatchet Gap to the Animas Mountains. Ideal desert car-camping, several miles off the highway on a little-used ranch road. But dreams came in rapid succession—recurring scenes of friends reproaching me as I turned to leave, always as I turned to leave— and early this morning I was awakened by the frantic yelping of coyotes and the helpless lowing of cattle in the surrounding creosote. Then, an hour before first light, a pickup truck sped by on the road, kicking up a pall of dust and conjuring images of danger and pursuit, death in the borderland.

The feeling has been slow to dissipate. As I walked along the ranch road early this morning, I still felt fatigued and disoriented. The air was dense and lifeless—no sound, no movement—and for a few minutes I had the sensation that our time here was at an end, that the earth had stopped turning and the sun had gone black, that the fate of the world was forever darkness and deepening chill.

Now that the light is coming up, however, my disquietude is receding. There is comfort, as always, in the familiar diurnal cycle of the planet. As dawn approaches, the vivid color fades from the eastern horizon. Red weakens to orange softens to yellow pales to white, and brightness spreads overhead like a door opening from a lighted room onto a darkened hallway. Finally sunlight strikes the colorful strata of the Big Hatchets, and a cactus wren calls from a cholla. It seems to be calling to me: the beautiful, brittle breaking of a new day.

At Antelope Wells, the most isolated crossing along the 1,933-mile border between the United States and Mexico, a barbed-wire fence separates the two nations, and a hinged ranch gate guards the crossing itself. I pull up and stop at the building on this side of the fence, and a U.S. customs inspector breaks off his conversation with one of his Mexican counterparts to see what I want.

Just driving to see what's at the end of the road, I tell him.

He nods; he's heard it before. He is a short Hispanic man in his mid-thirties, with tinted glasses, a pencil mustache, and a snub-nosed .38 in a holster on his hip. His name is Rudy, and his manner is taciturn. Nevertheless, the day is slow and we begin to chat in the shade of the carport that extends from the front of the United States Border Inspection Station. Inside the station another customs inspector is talking on a two-way radio and doing some paperwork.

I ask Rudy how many cars a day cross the border at Antelope Wells.

"We average about eight northbound a day. Maybe two or three times that many southbound."

As if on cue, a car approaches the crossing from the Mexican side. Rudy turns and watches it as it parks in front of the buildings on the other side of the fence. He doesn't look back until the driver shuts off the engine.

"But we don't care about the southbound cars," he says indifferently. "They're the Mexicans' problem."

With so little traffic, why is there a border crossing at Antelope Wells?

He shrugs. "It's an old crossing—it was established by President Grant."

He pauses. He doesn't like volunteering information, but this conversation, I can see him thinking, is harmless enough. "A few years ago there was some talk of closing it, but the New Mexico congressional delegation opposed that. Columbus and Antelope Wells are the only two crossings in New Mexico. When it opens, Santa Teresa will be the third."

I ask him if Antelope Wells is considered good duty.

"If you like solitude, it's great duty. If you don't, it's terrible."

I ask him if he likes it.

"Yeah. But I grew up on a ranch near Hachita, so I'm used to it."

Rudy and his wife—they have no children—have
lived here for about three and a half years. They shop
once a week, usually in Deming or Las Cruces, occasionally in Tucson. His wife doesn't work but stays at
home in their cinder-block house behind the inspection
station. He says she likes living at Antelope Wells.

I don't question what he says, but I also can't
help thinking that living here for three and a half years is
likely to engender some pretty strange behavior. Similar
to that engendered by living, for example, in Chaco
Canyon. I think about his wife, sitting alone in their cinder-block house all day.

Rudy is growing impatient with my questions
about life at Antelope Wells, so I ask if he knows the condition of the road through Coronado National Forest
and across the Peloncillo Mountains between New Mexico and Arizona, which I intend to drive tomorrow afternoon and about which I have heard conflicting reports.

"It's a good road," he says. "I haven't been over
it in a few years, but it's as good as the road you just
drove. The Forest Service maintains it real well."

The road reminds him of something. "Over there
in Cloverdale, on the New Mexico side, used to be a wild
place. Lots of outlaws. The Clanton gang, Johnny Ringo,
Black Jack Ketchum. They robbed trains and stagecoaches and ambushed smugglers coming up from Mexico, then sold the stuff themselves. Old man Clanton
finally got ambushed himself, down in Mexico. Anyway,
there was a cantina in Cloverdale where they went to
drink and raise hell."

Is the cantina still there?

He shakes his head. "One of the local ranchers stored hay in it for a while, but I think it's abandoned now. They took the old mahogany bar to a little place in Hachita. It had silver dollars and turquoise nuggets embedded in the wood under the glass top, and you could drink across the same bar as those outlaws did a long time ago."

Was that the place owned by Mrs. Been? I ask, mentioning by way of explanation that I read about her establishment in a book.

"Yeah. But she sold the building to a man from Deming about ten years ago. The building's still there, but I don't know what happened to the old bar. He might have taken it to Deming."

His partner, a tall Anglo in his early thirties, with a pack of Marlboros in his shirt pocket and a lighted cigarette in his hand, comes outside to join us. His name is Dwight, and, although he seems more affable than Rudy, he too wears dark glasses and carries a gun.

I ask them about an object I observed yesterday afternoon and early this morning in the sky east of Hachita. At first I thought it was an airplane, but it didn't move—just hovered in the sky above the border.

They laugh. "You didn't see anything," Dwight says. "You people come out to the desert and always think you see UFOs. You just imagined it."

"Yeah," says Rudy. "Or maybe it was a hot-air balloon from Deming."

They laugh some more, conspiratorially. I decide it might be wise to change the subject again.

I ask if they are ever called to assist the Border Patrol.

They shake their heads. "Our duty station is right here, at Antelope Wells," Rudy answers definitively. "We guard the crossing."

Any other duties?

"We take weather measurements."

Anything else?

"Nope. It's pretty quiet. Best job I ever had," Rudy says seriously. He stares at me from behind his dark glasses. My questions are beginning to annoy him or arouse his suspicion—maybe both.

"Coffee from eight to four. Tequila from four to eight," Dwight says with a laugh, breaking the momentary silence.

Dwight has been here for only a few months. I ask him if he likes it.

"Yeah, I do. I was stationed at Nogales before I transferred here. Nogales has six separate crossings—two vehicular, two pedestrian, a freight crossing, and the international airport. We worked sixteen-hour shifts, six days a week. Mandatory overtime. I'm glad to be out of there."

What's the busiest border crossing?

Dwight ponders for a minute. "Either El Paso or Calexico. El Paso gets . . . I think it's about thirty thousand vehicles and seventy thousand pedestrians a day."

As we talk, an elderly Mexican gentleman dressed in a white shirt, a satin tie, and a felt fedora walks across the border. Rudy and Dwight greet him in Spanish as he passes us to use the pay phone located on the outside wall of the station.

"That's Mr. Johnson," Dwight says after he again crosses into Mexico. "He's the Mexican immigration officer. He's been at Antelope Wells since 1948."

How many other people work on the Mexican side?

"They have three customs inspectors. Plus some cowboys from the local ranch live over there," he says, nodding toward the buildings on the Mexican side, set under some withered cottonwood trees.

The afternoon is beginning to wane; it is time for me to ease on down the road. I ask Rudy and Dwight if I may take their photograph in front of their duty station.

Both men stare at me sullenly; neither says anything. Their expressions are dour. The air is suddenly charged with tension. I have overstepped some invisible line, violated some unspoken taboo, threatened the secret, sacred anonymity of customs inspectors. I take the hint and say good-bye politely. They nod and watch as I turn my car around and start north toward Hachita. When I look in my rearview mirror, they are still watching.

There is no public road across the Animas Mountains, and I must retrace my route forty-five miles to Hachita and New Mexico 9 before turning west. As I drive slowly north, the sun seems to reach a stasis in the western sky, a warm breeze fills the car with the smell of creosote and desert wildflowers, and I find myself in a pensive mood.

In February 1978 I left family and friends on the East Coast to come to the Southwest. At that time I was a discontent, unemployed college graduate, and I drove west ostensibly to start work at Canyonlands National Park in southeastern Utah. But the job only provided a plausible cover for the move; in truth, I had visited the Four Corners area several times before and had been secretly biding my time until I could return. Something about the landscape of the desert Southwest—its empty vistas or its faultless skies or its brilliant light—had grabbed hold of my imagination and insistently, quietly pulled me back.

"Because it's clean," Ed Abbey wrote somewhere by way of explaining his attraction to the Southwest, a line I have always interpreted to mean the landscape's simple lines and geometric forms, and (if my interpretation is correct) a sentiment I have long shared.

A product of relatively homogeneous suburbs, I was also attracted by the region's ethnic and cultural diversity. Here were indigenous peoples still occupying their aboriginal lands; the descendants of conquistadors and Spanish colonists; and the myriad products of the hybridization, over the centuries, of those two groups—the mestizos of the southwestern United States and northern Mexico. I was intrigued by their customs and languages (so different from mine), excited to be a stranger in their midst.

And, finally, I had experienced the appeal—a peculiarly American phenomenon—of driving hundreds of miles over deserted highways and back roads, a feeling that those roads might lead anywhere and that one might discover, around the next curve, almost anything (a legendary ghost town, a clandestine drug deal). It is the euphoric feeling described with poetic imprecision by Jack Kerouac in *On the Road*, a feeling that the entire continent is waiting, beckoning. In retrospect I see clearly that this last is at heart a youthful impulse—the urge to strike out on one's own, to leave behind the routine and familiar, to live solely by one's wits. And when I was young, the Southwest is where I came to do exactly that.

West of Hachita the highway continues along the route of the old border railroad, crossing the continental divide (a low, grassy saddle between the Pyramid Mountains to the north and the Animas Mountains to the south) and passing through the dusty hamlet of Animas. Beyond Antelope Pass, away in Arizona, the massive escarpment of the Chiricahuas dominates the view, spreading darkly across the sky above the arid San Simon Valley. The prospect is daunting, even a little sinister. The escarpment is raked by deep canyons, and the mountains' late-afternoon shadow spreads slowly across the valley, eclipsing the light. There is, I think, a dark center to those mountains, a secret hollowness within them, a portal to another world.

As often happens, I find myself trying to imagine how this landscape—this particular landscape—has affected the people who have beheld and inhabited it. What of the Chiricahua Apaches, the bands of Cochise and Geronimo? For hundreds of years their nomadic existence revolved around these mountains and the other ranges in the area (the Peloncillos to the east and the Dragoons to the west). They camped near springs in the foothills, ventured from the mountains to hunt and raid, and retreated to them to avoid or ambush their enemies. But what did this place *mean* to them? When they viewed these mountains from a distance (under a full moon, say, or with the morning sun at their backs), what feelings welled within their hearts? And after their eventual surrender, after they were locked in railroad cars and exiled to Florida and Alabama, did images of the mountains haunt their sleep?

Driving down the San Simon Valley toward Douglas, I also find myself thinking about the first Europeans to traverse this country. In 1535 the four survivors of the Narváez expedition, led by the intrepid Alvar Núñez Cabeza de Vaca, skirted the western foothills of the Chiricahuas en route to Mexico City. Although Cabeza de Vaca's chronicle of their journey, written five years after the fact, makes passing reference to the Chiricahuas (the "massive mountains") and the local Indians, its value and appeal lie, not in the meager geographic and ethnographic information it contains, but rather in the story it tells. It is a condensed epic, a record of adventure, hardship, and survival, and one of the great tales to come out of the exploration of the New World.

Pámfilo de Narváez had been authorized by the King of Spain "to conquer and govern the provinces which should be encountered from the River of Palms [the Rio Grande] to the cape of Florida." In 1528, with four hundred men under his command, he sailed up the peninsula's west coast. Near Tampa Bay, however, Narváez decided to leave his ships to search inland for the legendary city of Apalachen. Hard months later the expedition foundered in the estuaries near the Apalachicola River. His men were sick with malaria and dysentery, and the Indians, hidden in the surrounding forest, harassed their movements with fusillades of arrows. In desperation the Spaniards constructed four wooden barges and paddled into the Gulf of Mexico.

Eventually the barge commanded by Cabeza de Vaca wrecked on Galveston Island. Cabeza de Vaca, separated from the other survivors and enslaved by the Indians who found him, eventually improved his lot by offering his services as a "wandering merchant," carrying trade goods between warring coastal and inland tribes. (Most historians believe he traveled as far as present-day Oklahoma on his missions.) In 1534 he was reunited with the only other survivors of the expedition—two Spaniards and the Moor Estevánico—who had been held by other native groups near the coast. The four then began their long overland trek to Mexico. They walked across Texas, southern New Mexico (probably crossing the Rio Grande somewhere near the site of present-day Hatch, north of Las Cruces), and southeastern Arizona. Along the way they came to be regarded as powerful shamans by the various Indian groups they contacted because of their success as faith healers. By the time they reached the Chiricahuas, they were accompanied by a huge entourage of natives seeking the benefits of their curative powers.

Cabeza de Vaca had always been a religious man, and his experiences affected him profoundly, enriching his faith and instilling in him a respect for the strange peoples he encountered. After he and his companions reached Mexico City, however, their reports of the wonders of the continent—mineral wealth, exotic animals, and stories of opulent, unseen cities to the north— inspired the Fray Marcos and Coronado expeditions and, eventually, the Spanish colonization of the American Southwest. The whole sad, irredeemable history of relations between Indians and Europeans begins, in this part of the world, with the innocent, miraculous journey of Cabeza de Vaca.

After a night's sleep and breakfast in the Gadsden Hotel in downtown Douglas, I set out to run some errands and renew my acquaintance with the town. Douglas was the western terminus of the border railroad, in an area that historically had close ties to New Mexico's Boot Heel. From Cloverdale, for example, the Clanton gang rode across the Peloncillo Mountains and into the mythology of the Old West when its members battled the Earp brothers—Wyatt, Morgan, and Virgil—and Doc Holliday for control of Tombstone, Arizona. (During the gunfight near the OK Corral in October 1881 at least two of the Clanton gang were unarmed. Wyatt and Doc Holliday, never well liked by the townspeople, were eventually indicted for murder and forced to flee Arizona Territory. So much for the mythology of the Old West.)

Douglas enjoyed its boom slightly later, in the early years of this century, when the Phelps Dodge smelters in town worked twenty-four hours a day to refine the copper ore coming from the mining district near Bisbee. Agua Prieta, the site of Pancho Villa's defeat in 1915, similarly grew up across the border. Today Douglas is a shell of its former self, its smelters doomed by the Clean Air Act and the Environmental Protection Agency, but Agua Prieta, located outside the territorial jurisdiction of the United States, continues to thrive as a mining town and port of entry and, most recently, a location for *maquiladoras*.

Downtown Douglas is sleepy this quiet weekday morning. As I cruise down main street (Avenue G), however, I notice two large, colorful murals painted on the sides of adjacent buildings and facing each other across a small vacant lot. I circle and park my car in the alley behind. A few minutes later, as I am photographing the murals, an elderly couple approaches me.

"Perdóneme, señor. Por favor. ¿Viene de Nuevo Mexico?" the man asks eagerly. He has seen my license plate.

Sí, I respond, though my Spanish is too limited to continue the conversation for long. Pero no hablo Español muy bien.

"Ah. Are you from New Mexico?" he asks again in Spanish-inflected English.

Yes.

"From Albuquerque?"

No, I tell him, Santa Fe. But I lived in Albuquerque for three years.

"Is Albuquerque a nice town?"

Their names are Pedro and Maria Armendariz, and they have recently moved to Douglas from San Francisco, where they lived and worked for forty-six years. It is a homecoming of sorts, as Pedro grew up in Agua Prieta in the years before World War II. He is a slight man, with a ready smile, a gimpy leg, and a face creased by hard work.

Maria is from Guatemala and has the broad face and features of the Maya Indians. As a young woman she came to this country to work in a Guatemalan consulate; she has lived here ever since. Nevertheless, today she is wearing a *huipil*—a cotton blouse—and a long skirt with bright, embroidered patterns, the clothing of her girlhood. Her manner is shy and her smile warm, but her eyes have a sad, weary look about them—the look of one who has seen the cruelty of which the world is capable.

"We're both citizens now," Maria says proudly, though I haven't asked.

Their move to Douglas has been disappointing. The climate is hotter than they like, and the town itself is not the bustling commercial center Pedro remembers.

"Back then Douglas was a nice town," he says fondly. "Lots of restaurants and a movie theater downtown. Lots of pretty girls," he says with a mischievous look in his eyes, as Maria smiles and chides him gently in Spanish.

"But now." He nods toward the empty buildings downtown. "No place to eat anymore except the hotel. No movie theater. There's nothing here anymore. And Agua Prieta has grown big and dirty. It's not like it used to be. We've been thinking about moving to Albuquerque. Is it a nice town?" he asks again.

I tell them that it is a no-nonsense, working town; that housing is relatively inexpensive; that it is cooler than Douglas; and that although I don't know them well, I think they would like it.

"Are there a lot of Spanish people there?" Pedro asks.

I tell them yes, and I add that many people in Albuquerque speak Spanish much better than I.

"I think we'll visit. Maybe this week," he says. "We might ride the bus."

I tell them that a car would make their visit easier, as Albuquerque is not known for its convenient public transportation. I look at their car, which they have parked behind mine in the alley. It is an old Toyota station wagon with wooden panels on the side. It is immaculate, and the tires are new.

I think your car will make it, I tell them.

Pedro smiles, pleased that I have noticed. I imagine him in his driveway, tinkering under the hood, then washing and waxing the car.

He nods and looks at Maria. "All right. We'll drive."

With that settled, we chat for another ten or fifteen minutes, discussing Pedro's work in a shipyard in San Francisco and Maria's infrequent visits to Guatemala. The border sun, high overhead, bathes us with light and warmth.

"Well, we'll let you get back to what you're doing," Pedro says finally. "Thank you for talking to us."

I smile at them. It has been my pleasure, I say, feeling in my heart that is true. Good luck to you, I say, though at the same time I am thinking, People like you should not need luck. The world should take care of you.

▼ The Boot Heel ▼

I drive east from Douglas on a graded dirt road that the local chamber of commerce has dubbed the Geronimo Trail. The road parallels the border for about twenty miles, then angles northeast to cross the Peloncillo Mountains into New Mexico. In 1886 Geronimo surrendered in Skeleton Canyon in the Peloncillos after fending off and evading the U.S. Army and local vigilantes for ten years. Geronimo was the last Apache headman of stature to make peace, and his surrender effectively ended the Indian wars in the Southwest.

Before his surrender, however, Geronimo frustrated his pursuers by crossing and recrossing the border between the United States and Mexico, often taking refuge in the rugged canyons of the Sierra Madre in northern Sonora. Thinking about that, I am reminded of how recent (and arbitrary) a creation the border is. For thousands of years before European contact Indians moved freely along these desert ridges and washes. Even after colonization this entire area was of a piece—a province of New Spain and, later, Mexico. It is only for the past century and a half, since the Gadsden Purchase, that a boundary between two sovereign nations has divided it, a boundary that, when it was established, followed latitudinal, not topographic or cultural, lines.

Of course, the establishment of the border initiated a process of differentiation between people on opposite sides of the fence, a process that continues to this day. Still, despite the existence of the border, despite the construction of barricades, crossings, and ports of entry, despite the efforts of the Border Patrol and the

Customs Service, people like Pedro and Maria Armendariz still find their way across, bringing with them their language, their memories, their dreams of a better life.

After crossing the San Bernardino Valley, the road climbs toward the Peloncillos, and soon it is winding along Cottonwood Creek into the mountains. Mesquite, agave, and ocotillo give way to cottonwood, sycamore, and Chihuahua pine, which yield, as the road climbs above the creek bed, to manzanita, scrub oak, and alligator juniper. Pink- and dun-colored rhyolitic walls and pinnacles spotted with phosphorescent lime-green lichen tower above me. The canyon is not as spectacular as Cave Creek Canyon in the Chiricahuas but is cut from the same rock and exhibits the same eerie beauty.

Rudy, the sullen customs inspector, was wrong. As it climbs, the road grows ever rougher, ever rockier, and before long I find myself thinking, If it gets any worse, I'll turn around. But the promise of what lies around the next curve draws me onward, and I creep and crawl ahead, the skid plate (or crankcase?) under my Honda occasionally scraping a protruding rock. Finally I see, half a mile distant, the saddle through which the road passes. At the divide, just across the state line, I pull over, stop, and climb out of the car to stretch and breathe.

Low rocky summits stair-step to the northeast, and in the opposite direction, across the border, the peaks of the Sierra Madre rise mysteriously in a desert haze. To the west the Perilla Mountains shimmer above the San Bernardino Valley, while to the east, beyond Clanton

▼ The Boot Heel ▼

Draw, soft, grass-mantled foothills roll up to the ridgeline scarp of the Animas Mountains.

Although the land everywhere appears deserted, on this quiet afternoon I can sense, through some invisible medium, the presence of the people who have inhabited it over the course of the centuries. A restless, milling crowd of ghosts, each acting out a life apart from the others, each trapped in a capsule of time. Faint and indistinct, speaking a babel of languages, their voices drift on the breeze from the canyon below.

Whatever their reasons for coming here, all of those people responded to the hardships and beauty of the land, and all contributed their energy to the peculiar spirit of this place. And the process continues through us, the living. By choice or chance or necessity we come to be for a time in a particular place; we pass a portion of our lives in that place; and through our work and love and pain we expend ourselves upon it, claim it as our own. And in the process of claiming that place, that small piece of the earth, we help to transform the planet. What is history, after all, but an amalgamation of our life stories?

I came to the Southwest as a young man, drawn by an ancient westward urging and my own romantic notions of what it means to be young in America. I came of age here, in this desert place, and images of its landscapes—subtle and garish, intimate and vast—crystallized in my psyche. They became a lattice, a trellis around which are twined my closest memories—of friends, youth, wildness, the heartbreaking beauty of the world.

But much time has passed already. I am older now, and this place, once so foreign, has become my home. It contains me—my hands' work and common personal history—and in some sense I incorporate it. Like blood or marrow it is a part of me, constituent and essential, though most of the time I am not even aware of its presence, so deeply is it embedded in my life. But then suddenly, unexpectedly, I experience a moment of awakening (like this one, on a bright October afternoon in the Peloncillo Mountains), when I see the world as for the first time, the landscape vivid and new, and I feel blessed again by the good fortune that has brought me here. How, I ask myself, can I think of going elsewhere? Of leaving this place dearest to me? And I shiver then, for time is fleeting, and who can say what will happen with the next revolution of the planet, where events and circumstances will carry us, and whether, if I leave this place, I will ever return.

Author's Note

This book represents my attempt to describe and evoke a part of my life in the Southwest. Although it embodies my idiosyncratic point of view, my intention was not to inflict or provoke, but only to write honestly.

With respect to the people I encountered during my travels, I was struck not only by their apparent differences, but also by their fundamental similarities. Despite our variety, we are, all of us, in the end, very much alike. And it is that coincidence of the strange and familiar that I find intriguing and that I struggled to capture in these pieces.

Although all of the people described in this book are or were real, I have changed some names and other details in order to protect the privacy of the individuals concerned.

Acknowledgments

I wish to thank the various people who appear in these pages under their real names or under pseudonyms. Without them the book would be a dull affair indeed.

Dave and Peg Johnson, Peter and Susan Schultz, and Valerie Martin provided friendship and encouragement during the years I worked on this book, and to them I extend my heartfelt thanks. My colleagues in writing workshops at the Universities of Iowa and New Mexico read early drafts of several chapters, and their thoughtful and provocative comments helped me to understand what I was trying to say. Roberta Rusch read the entire manuscript upon completion and, through her incisive but gentle criticism, urged me to focus my vision and sharpen my prose.

I owe a special debt to my small circle of friends from Chaco Canyon: Dan Steed, Frank Buono, Tom Tanaka, and, especially, Randy Morrison, who, in addition to long evenings of chess and whiskey all those years ago, gave me the benefit of his acumen by reading and commenting on several chapters.

I gratefully acknowledge the following for permission to quote portions of the indicated works:

Dr. Victor Westphall, for permission to quote lines from *What Are THEY Doing to MY World?* (New York: Cornwall Books, 1981) and *David's Story: A Casualty of Vietnam* (Springer, New Mexico: Center for the Advancement of Human Dignity/Vietnam Veterans Chapel, 1981).

The Merton Legacy Trust, for permission to quote lines from "Christ in the Desert" (Abiquiu, New Mexico: Monastery of Christ in the Desert, 1967).

Brandt and Brandt Literary Agents, Inc., for permission to reprint "Daniel Boone," from *A Book of Americans*, by Stephen Vincent Benét, copyright 1933 Stephen Vincent Benét, copyright renewed (c) 1961 by Rosemary Carr Benét.

Hal Leonard Corporation, for permission to quote lyrics from "Annie," words and music by Eric Clapton, Ronnie Lane, and Katie Lambert. Copyright © 1978 Slim Chance Music and Eric Patrick Clapton. All rights on behalf of Slim Chance Music administered by WB Music Corp. All rights on behalf of Eric Patrick Clapton administered by Unichappell Music, Inc. International copyright secured. All rights reserved.

Mr. Frank Waters, for permission to quote lines from *Masked Gods: Navaho and Pueblo Ceremonialism*, 2d ed. (Athens, Ohio: Swallow Press/Ohio University Press, 1950, reprinted 1991).